# The Books  for Spiritual Growth

*Dick B*

*2005*

## Other Titles by Dick B.

*Dr. Bob's Library: Books for Twelve Step Growth*

*Anne Smith's Journal, 1933-1939: A.A.'s Principles of Success*

*The Oxford Group & Alcoholics Anonymous:*
    *A Design for Living That Works*

*The Akron Genesis of Alcoholics Anonymous*

*New Light on Alcoholism: The A.A. Legacy from Sam Shoemaker*

*Courage to Change* (with Bill Pittman)

*The Good Book and The Big Book: A.A.'s Roots in the Bible*

*That Amazing Grace:*
    *The Role of Clarence and Grace S. in Alcoholics Anonymous*

*Good Morning!:*
    *Quiet Time, Morning Watch, Meditation, and Early A.A.*

*Turning Point:*
    *A History of Early A.A.'s Spiritual Roots and Successes*

*HOPE!: The Story of Geraldine D., Alina Lodge & Recovery*

*Utilizing Early A.A.'s Spiritual Roots for Recovery Today*

# The Books Early AAs Read
## for
# Spiritual Growth

## Dick B.

**Paradise Research Publications, Inc.**
Kihei, Maui, Hawaii

Paradise Research Publications, Inc., P.O. Box 837, Kihei, HI
96753-0837

This Paradise Research Publications Seventh Edition is published
by arrangement with Good Book Publishing Company, P.O. Box
837, Kihei, Maui, HI 96753-0837

Cover design by: Lili Crawford, Maui Cyber Design

The publication of this volume does not imply affiliation with nor
approval or endorsement from Alcoholics Anonymous World
Services, Inc.

ISBN: 1-885803-26-5

(Earlier editions published by Glen Abbey Books, Good Book
Publishing Company, and Paradise Research Publications, Inc.)

Library of Congress Catalog Card Number: 98-92159

To Charles Mau and the Kathryn McManaman Mau Trust

# Contents

# Foreword

After the first meeting between Bill W. and Dr. Bob in Akron in 1935, they commenced an intensive exploration of the spiritual principles that would help alcoholics overcome their addiction. They attended meetings of the Oxford Group followers who met regularly at the home of T. Henry and Clarace Williams. Until Bill and Bob started bringing in "recruits," none of the others shared alcoholism as one of their personal problems.

Through the summer of 1935, Bill and Bob also met several times a week at Henrietta Seiberling's house. Their conversations often went on until late in the evening. Though not an alcoholic, she shared in the intense effort out of concern for Bill and Bob and as part of her own spiritual growth.

All this raises an interesting question: What did these non-alcoholics have that made Bill and Bob so eager to plumb their thoughts and to share experiences with them? Having myself attended some of the same Oxford Group meetings and, as the son of Henrietta, had many close, sharing conversations with her, I can think of no better way to recapture their spiritual inspiration than to turn to the books they read that were among the sources of their inspiration. Fortunately, it is now much easier to do this, thanks to the untiring work of Dick B., resulting, among other things, in his monumental publication of the list of readings from which A.A.'s founders and their friends drew healing spiritual power.

JOHN F. SEIBERLING

Akron, Ohio
August 5, 1998

ix

# Preface to the Seventh Edition

Over eight years ago, the author began researching the sources of A.A.'s spiritual ideas. From that work have emerged *Dr. Bob's Library, Anne Smith's Journal: 1933-1939, New Light on Alcoholism: The A.A. Legacy from Sam Shoemaker, The Akron Genesis of Alcoholics Anonymous, The Oxford Group & Alcoholics Anonymous: A Design for Living That Works, Courage to Change* (with Bill Pittman), *The Good Book and the Big Book: A.A.'s Roots in the Bible, That Amazing Grace: The Role of Clarence and Grace S. in Alcoholics Anonymous*; *Good Morning!: Quiet Time, Morning Watch, Meditation, and Early A.A.*; *Turning Point: A History of Early A.A.'s Spiritual Roots and Successes*; and *Utilizing Early A.A.'s Spiritual Roots for Recovery Today*. These eleven other titles deal with the various places, people, and writings from which A.A. spiritual ideas sprang. And out of the research for these books has come a clear picture of the actual literature that was studied by the founders of Alcoholics Anonymous as they put together their program of recovery—embodied in the Big Book as their text book and in the Twelve Steps as the actual recovery program they followed.

Still more work needs to be done. The author proposes to write several pamphlets which present in very simple form each of the contributions made to A.A. by its spiritual sources. The pamphlets will show how A.A.'s spiritual legacy can be used today to achieve the high degree of success (75% to 93%) that A.A. pioneers attained in the 1930's and early 1940's.

In his travels and communications, the author has encountered a host of people who are searching for the actual source books, collecting them, and reading them. He felt this present book would be useful to their quest and would become a resource book for scholars, historians, and archivists who continue to research and write on the ingredients of the spiritual solution developed by the early AAs before their Big Book and Twelve Steps went to print.

For a detailed authentication of the points we make, we refer the reader to our other titles mentioned above. Publication details about them are contained in the Bibliography of this present title. And the other titles contain ample footnotes, appendices, and bibliographies to support the statements and conclusions set forth in this present work.

# Acknowledgements

We refer the reader to our other titles for a complete accreditation of the many who have contributed to our research and writing.

Here we gratefully list: My son, Ken, for editorial, research, and computer assistance; the Rev. Dr. Richard McCandless, Sue Smith Windows, and Robert and Betty Smith for information on Dr. Bob and Anne Smith; John F. Seiberling, Dorothy Seiberling, and Mary Seiberling Huhn for information on Henrietta Seiberling; Dorothy Williams Culver for information on T. Henry and Clarace Williams; the Rev. Norman Vincent Peale and Nell Wing for information on Bill and Lois Wilson; Grace Snyder and Clarence Snyder's sponsees for information on Clarence Snyder; Frank M., Paul B., Ray G., Paul L., Gail L., Dale M., Dave S., Edie U., Danny W, Berry W., and Bob and Fay W. for archival material; Mel B., Charlie B., Dennis C., Geraldine D., Mary D., Earl H., Mitch K., Dr. Ernest Kurtz, Joe McQ., Merton M., Charlie P., Bill P., Bob R., Bill R., Ray R., Eddie S., Sally S., and Bruce W. for their research; for information on Shoemaker: Marjory Zoet Bankson, the Rev. David Else, the Rev. Paul Everett, Mrs. W. Irving Harris, Nickie Shoemaker Haggart, the Rev. Greg Hammond, Dr. Karen Plavan, Dr. Norman Vincent Peale, Sally Shoemaker Robinson, and the Rev. David Sack; the Rev. Harry Almond, Kenneth Belden, Terry Blair, the Rev. Howard Blake, Sydney Cook, Morgan Firestone, Charles Haines, Michael Henderson, James Houck, the Rev. T. Willard Hunter, Michael Hutchinson, Garth D. Lean, Dr. Morris Martin, Dr. R. C. Mowat, Eleanor Forde Newton, James Draper Newton, Richard Ruffin, L. Parks Shipley, Sr., George Vondermuhll, Jr., and Ted Watt for information on the Oxford Group.

The following made valuable resources available: A.A. General Services Archives; the archives at Dr. Bob's Home and at Founders Day in Akron; Stepping Stones Archives; Episcopal Church Archives; Hartford Seminary Archives; New York University Archives; the Oxford Group archives at their London book centre, the main O.G. archives at Tirley, and M.R.A. archives in Washington, D.C.; the church archives at Calvary Episcopal Church in New York and in Pittsburgh; Bierce Library at Akron University; Rockefeller Library at Brown University; Enoch Pratt Library in Baltimore; Golden Gate Baptist Seminary Library in Tiburon; Graduate Theological Union Library in Berkeley; Princeton Public Library; San Francisco Theological Seminary Library in San Anselmo; Corte Madera Public Library; and the Kahului, Kihei, Makawao, and Wailuku Public Libraries in Maui, Hawaii.

Much has come to the author from A.A. friends and acquaintances: David A., Larry B., Dennis C., Jim F., Steve F., Chris K., Ray M., Dale M., Wally P., Bob P., Grace S., George T., Edie U., Bruce W., Chuck W., Danny W., as well as The Pittsburgh Experiment and Faith at Work. God Bless them all!

# Introduction

From what written sources did Alcoholics Anonymous derive its spiritual ideas? Today we can answer that question in almost complete detail. We can also reasonably conclude that there really were six major spiritual sources which provided the information early AAs borrowed.

There is an excellent book by Mel B., titled *New Wine: The Spiritual Roots of the Twelve Step Miracle* (Minnesota: Hazelden, 1991). In that book, Mel B. concisely spells out some possible roots for A.A. ideas; and some of the literature which Mel mentions *was* read and used by A.A. founders.

Others have also named specific sources for A.A. ideas. Dr. Bob was emphatic that A.A.'s basic ideas came from the Bible—the "Good Book," as he called it. Bill Wilson was equally definite that A.A.'s program was derived largely from the Oxford Group, "led in America," as Bill put it, by The Reverend Samuel Moor Shoemaker, Jr. A.A.'s pioneer, Clarence S., put the two sources in perspective when he stated: "We owe our origin to the Oxford Group. . . . We had a program presented to us that worked. . . . Everything in this program came from the Bible." (See Dick B., *That Amazing Grace: The Role of Clarence and Grace S. in Alcoholics Anonymous*, p. 43.) Others have pointed to Professor William James, Dr. Carl G. Jung, James Allen, Oswald Chambers, Glenn Clark, Henry Drummond, Mary Baker Eddy, Harry Emerson Fosdick, Emmet Fox, E. Stanley Jones, *The Upper Room*, Christian classics, and several additional religious writers.

1

Some have strongly suggested that the Twelve Steps, and A.A.'s Big Book as well, were "divinely inspired." And the author would be the last to reject this thesis, given the spiritual posture from which Bill W., Dr. Bob, and the other founders were coming. Most of these pioneers had, in biblical terms, the spiritual standing, as children of God, to receive divine revelation; and all firmly believed in "Guidance," the Oxford Group term for Guidance by the "Holy Spirit."

But the founders of Alcoholics Anonymous mentioned, and the literature which they read contained, specific words and ideas which can be traced into A.A. literature—written materials which did not come from divine revelation, though the founders may have been guided to use them. The Big Book's words and ideas themselves came mostly from specific, written sources.

Thus Dr. Bob and his wife often mentioned the Bible as the main source of A.A.'s ideas. So did Henrietta Seiberling, T. Henry and Clarace Williams, and Clarence S. Later, to a limited degree, so did Bill Wilson. So do A.A.'s Conference Approved histories. Many oldtimers spoke specifically about *The Upper Room*, Oswald Chambers' *My Utmost for His Highest*, *The Runner's Bible*, the Glenn Clark books, the E. Stanley Jones books, James Allen's *As a Man Thinketh*, Henry Drummond's *The Greatest Thing in the World*, the Emmet Fox books, Harold Begbie's books, two Lewis Browne books, William James, Carl Jung, the Oxford Group literature, and the Sam Shoemaker books. Bill Wilson often remarked that no one "invented" A.A. Its ideas were "borrowed," he said, from ancient and universal sources—the common property of mankind. And Bill often cited the clergy (possibly including Dr. Frank N. D. Buchman, Father Ed Dowling, Father John Ford, the Rev. W. Irving Harris, the Rev. Norman Vincent Peale, the Rev. Harry Emerson Fosdick, the Rev. Samuel M Shoemaker, Jr., and the Rev. Walter Tunks) and religion itself–as prime sources of the A.A. spiritual ideas that were borrowed.

The difficulty for scholars is that no A.A. personage who wrote prior to the publication of the Big Book in 1939 was at all specific as to what A.A. ideas came from what specific sources. To be sure, Dr. Bob did mention Jesus's Sermon on the Mount, the Book of James, and 1 Corinthians 13 in the Bible. His wife, Anne Ripley Smith, wrote very specific ideas in her spiritual journal that cited Christian literature and Bible verses; and these ideas can be identified in present A.A. writings. Bill Wilson, the author of the Twelve Steps, and of almost the entirety of the Big Book, seldom got specific but did mention the "Apostle James" as a favorite. He also declared the importance of "Corinthians," as he put it.

Hence the importance of what early AAs read has more to do with learning *precisely* what spiritual tools they used for recovery and *precisely* how they maintained and grew in their spiritual condition than with whether their reading contributed to this or that specific idea that Bill Wilson incorporated into the Twelve Steps and the Big Book.

Anne Ripley Smith, Dr. Bob's wife, wrote several times in the journal she assembled between 1933 and 1939 that God can guide reading; that reading is an essential part of the Christian's diet; that the Christian should read that which can be assimilated and will be nourishing; that if he or she does not know what books to read, that person should see some one who is "surrendered" and who is mature in the "Groups" (the Oxford Groups); and that he or she should see the minister for books other than those Anne specifically mentioned. Her specific references to *Christians* can be understood in light of the fact that the Oxford Group was also called *A First Century Christian Fellowship*, that early AAs were an integral part of the Oxford Group, and that they called themselves a *Christian Fellowship*.

Anne frequently read from her spiritual journal to those who were being helped in the Smith home at 855 Ardmore in Akron,

Ohio. On the basis of much research, we now believe that Bill Wilson was one of those who heard Anne read from her journal while he was living at the Smith home for three months and also on those occasions when he later visited Dr. Bob's home with some frequency in A.A.'s formative years. In fact, Bill several times mentioned the reading that Anne did during morning quiet time—reading from the Bible and from other spiritual literature.

Interestingly, Anne's ideas about the importance of, and necessity for obtaining spiritual growth through, spiritual reading seem to have flowed into page 87 of the Big Book, which discusses morning meditation, morning prayer, and morning devotion. A.A.'s Big Book (its basic textbook) says:

> There are many helpful books also. Suggestions about these may be obtained from one's priest, minister, or rabbi. Be quick to see where religious people are right. Make use of what they offer.

In this context, therefore, we set forth the specific literature which our research has now revealed with some clarity to have been the literature early AAs read. Their studies were guided by Dr. Bob, Anne Smith—his wife, Henrietta Seiberling, T. Henry and Clarace Williams, Oxford Group members, Reverend Samuel Moor Shoemaker, Jr., and Shoemaker's associates at Calvary Episcopal Church in New York and in the Oxford Group business men's team, some of whose members spent much time, in pre-Big Book days, with Bill Wilson. As our research has continued, we have also had access to a large number of suggested reading lists in circulation during A.A.'s formative years. These were published by the Oxford Group in Great Britain; by *The Calvary Evangel*, Sam Shoemaker's parish publication, which was virtually the "house organ" for the Oxford Group in America; and by Glenn Clark, whose books were widely read in early A.A. Our summary of the six major sources from which all these spiritual contributions can be pinpointed can be found in our latest title: *Utilizing Early A.A.'s Spiritual Roots for Recovery Today.*

We hasten to point out what Dr. Bob, Anne, Bill, Lois, Henrietta, T. Henry and Clarace seem very definitely to have believed: Their reading was guided by God!

# 1

# The Bible:
# "The Main Source Book of All"

There can be little doubt that in early Akron A.A.—A.A. before the Big Book was published—the Bible was the main source of the basic ideas from which A.A.'s ideas sprang. The Bible was read by members in their homes. It was read at Quiet Times. It was read at the opening of meetings. It was the topic of the daily devotionals such as *The Upper Room* which were read each day in Quiet Time and at meetings. And it was the subject of almost all the spiritual literature AAs read—Oxford Group literature, Shoemaker literature, and the other books they read, books by James Allen, Harold Begbie, Brother Lawrence, Oswald Chambers, Glenn Clark, Henry Drummond, Mary Baker Eddy, Harry Emerson Fosdick, Emmet Fox, Toyohiko Kagawa, E. Stanley Jones, and the others.

In his last major address to Alcoholics Anonymous, Dr. Bob said of the early days:

At that point, our stories didn't amount to anything to speak of. When we started in on Bill D., we had no Twelve Steps, either; we had no Traditions. But we were convinced that the answer to our problems was in the Good Book. To some of us older ones, the parts we found absolutely essential were the

Sermon on the Mount, the thirteenth chapter of First
Corinthians, and the Book of James.

Dr. Bob modestly added:

> It wasn't until 1938 that the teachings and efforts and studies
> that had been going on were crystallized in the form of the
> Twelve Steps. I didn't write the Twelve Steps. I had nothing
> to do with the writing of them. But I think I probably had
> something to do with them indirectly. After my June 10th
> episode, Bill came to live at our house and stayed for about
> three months. There was hardly a night that we didn't sit up
> until two or three o'clock, talking. It would be hard for me to
> conceive that, during these nightly discussions around our
> kitchen table, nothing was said that influenced the writing of
> the Twelve Steps. We already had the basic ideas, though not
> in terse and tangible form. We got them, as I said, as a result
> of our study of the Good Book. We must have had them.
> Since then, we have learned from experience that they are
> very important in maintaining sobriety. We were maintaining
> sobriety—therefore, we must have had them.

At early A.A. meetings, the Bible was frequently read, and
at some length. In our title, Dick B., *The Akron Genesis of
Alcoholics Anonymous*, Newton ed. (Kihei, HI: Paradise Research
Publications, Inc., 1997), at pages 189-190, we quote from
statements by Alex M., Wally G., and Earl T., who recalled how
Dr. Bob, Dick S., and Bill D. [A.A. Number 3] all read passages
from the Bible at the earliest A.A. meetings and talked about its
relevance to the everyday life of those present. A.A. Conference
approved literature points to the reading of the Bible by Anne
Smith to Dr. Bob and to Bill Wilson. It also states that the Bible
was stressed as reading material in early A.A.

It was Bill Wilson who said, when he was interviewing T.
Henry and Clarace Williams in later years, that when he came to

Akron, he began to see the problem in light of the Bible's solution. He declared:

> I learned a great deal from you people [T. Henry and Clarace Williams, whom he was interviewing], from the Smiths themselves, and from Henrietta [Seiberling]. I hadn't looked in the Bible, up to this time at all. You see, I had the [conversion] experience first and then this rushing around to help drunks and nothing happened.

As we stated on page 80 of our book, *Anne Smith's Journal: 1933-1939* (San Rafael, CA: Paradise Research Publications, 1994), Anne wrote the following about Bible study at pages 16 and 48 of her journal:

> Of course the Bible ought to be the main Source Book of all. No day ought to pass without reading it. Read until some passage comes that "hits" you. Then pause and meditate over its meaning for your life. Begin reading the Bible with the Book of Acts and follow up with the Gospels and then the Epistles of Paul. Let "Revelation" alone for a while. The Psalms ought to be read and the Prophets.

Sam Shoemaker, to whom Bill Wilson gave the most credit for A.A. ideas, was known by his associates as a "Bible Christian." Sam frequently wrote about the importance of daily Bible study. As we discuss in Dick B., *The Oxford Group & Alcoholics Anonymous: A Design for Living That Works* (Kihei, HI: Paradise Research Publications, 1998), at page 251, Shoemaker wrote:

> The chief thing I want to emphasize about our use of the Bible is not so much the way each of us shall pursue our study of it, as the setting apart of a definite time each morning for this, together with prayer. . . . the results will justify the effort. . . .

Read and know the Bible, and all else, including public worship, will fall in its place.

Dr. Frank N. D. Buchman, founder of the Oxford Group, to which Bill Wilson attributed A.A. ideas, was said to have been "soaked in the Bible." His recipe for Bible-reading was, "Read accurately, interpret honestly, apply drastically." And the Reverend Sherwood Sunderland Day said very simply of Buchman's Oxford Group ideas: "The principles of 'The Oxford Group' are the principles of the Bible." [See our discussion in *The Oxford Group & Alcoholics Anonymous* at pages 9-13 and 249-53.]

In a little-remembered remark Bill Wilson made in his lecture at Yale University Summer School of Alcohol Studies, on August 3, 1944, Bill said:

> For a great many of us have taken to reading the Bible. It could not have been presented at first, but sooner or later in his second, third, or fourth year, the A.A. will be found reading his Bible, quite as often—or more—as he will a standard psychological work [See discussion in Dick B., *Dr. Bob's Library* (San Rafael, CA: Paradise Research Publications, 1994), pp. 10-11].

In *But, For the Grace of God . . .*, the author, Wally P., discussed a group of pamphlets published by "AA of Akron." Wally P. stated the pamphlets were written by Evan W., a former editor of the *Akron Beacon Journal*. Wally said Dr. Bob had asked Evan to write these "blue collar A.A." pamphlets to present the program in its most basic terms. Wally quoted a letter from Evan W. which stated that one of the pamphlets "has been highly popular throughout the country." That pamphlet—(probably) *A Manual for Alcoholics Anonymous*—contained a statement on its cover that it was written and edited by members of Alcoholics Anonymous of Akron, Ohio; and the statement certainly implies that it contains materials from a large number of persons whose sobriety dated back to 1935, 1936, and 1937.

The sixth, revised edition of *A Manual for Alcoholics Anonymous* contains this statement on p. 8:

> There is the Bible that you haven't opened for years. Get acquainted with it. Read it with an open mind. You will find things that will amaze you. You will be convinced that certain passages were written with you in mind. Read the Sermon on the Mount (Matthew V, VI, and VII). Read St. Paul's inspired essay on love (I Corinthians XIII). Read the Book of James. Read the Twenty-Third and Ninety-First Psalms. These readings are brief but so important.

Taken as a whole, the A.A. of Akron pamphlets are filled with Bible quotations. In our revised edition of Dick B., *The Good Book and The Big Book: A.A.'s Roots in the Bible*, Bridge Builders ed. (Kihei, HI: Paradise Research Publications, Inc., 1997), we quote in detail and at length from the various references in the pamphlets to segments of the Bible deemed important by the A.A. pioneers (See pp. 20-24).

To understand the biblical foundation of A.A., one needs to study Jesus's sermon on the mount (Matthew Chapters Five to Seven) in detail. Bill W. and Dr. Bob *both* said that Jesus's sermon on the mount set forth A.A.'s basic philosophy. In that sermon, one needs to look in the Beatitudes for many A.A. spiritual principles; in the entire sermon for specific sources of certain Steps; and in Matthew Chapter Five for A.A. principles of honesty, prayer, reconciliation, and love of one's neighbor (and even enemy). Matthew Chapter Six contains sources of some A.A. slogans. The Lord's Prayer (a part of Jesus's Sermon) sets forth ideas borrowed by AAs and concerning doing God's will and forgiveness. Chapter Seven of Matthew proclaims that doing the will of God is a condition of entry "into the kingdom of heaven," as Jesus taught it. Even the A.A. focus on anonymity as a spiritual principle may well have come from Matthew 6:1-7 and 6:16-18. Many surviving words and verses in today's A.A. come directly from the Book of James—the book that was so popular among AAs that early members wished to call the fellowship the "James Club." Moreover, the so-called "love" chapter in 1 Corinthians 13 was accorded great importance by both Bill W. and Dr. Bob.

The importance of the Bible as the main subject of early A.A. reading is perhaps best symbolized by the fact that Dr. Bob donated his Bible, with appropriate inscription, to A.A. Group No. 1, the King School Group, in Akron. And we personally observed during attendance there at an A.A. meeting, that Dr. Bob's Bible is still placed on the lectern at the beginning of each meeting of the King School Group of Alcoholics Anonymous in Akron.

# 2

# Dr. Bob's Reading
# and Recommendations

In his last major address to A.A., Dr. Bob made some comments
about his reading. He said of Bill and himself:

> We had both been associated with the Oxford Group, Bill in
> New York, for five months, and I in Akron, for two and a
> half years. Bill had acquired their idea of service. I had not,
> but I had done an immense amount of reading they had
> recommended. *I had refreshed my memory of the Good Book,
> and I had had excellent training in that as a youngster. . . .*
> (emphasis added).
>
> I'm somewhat allergic to work, but I felt that I should
> continue to increase my familiarity with the Good Book and
> also should read a good deal of standard literature, possibly
> of a scientific nature. So I did cultivate the habit of reading.
> I think I'm not exaggerating when I say I have probably
> averaged an hour a day for the last 15 years.

Dr. Bob had something else to say in his personal story which can
be found in each edition of the Big Book. Dr. Bob's statement has
caused the author to plumb some new materials that put a different
light on Dr. Bob's youthful training in the Bible, prayer,
meditation, and Christian reading. The materials also indicate Dr.

Bob's involvement in some activities which had nothing to do with
the Oxford Group, but which did have a good deal to do with
some of the practices carried on in early Akron A.A.

First, here is what Dr. Bob said:

> From childhood through high school I was more or less
> forced to go to church, Sunday School and evening service,
> Monday night *Christian Endeavor* and sometimes to
> Wednesday evening prayer meeting (Big Book First Edition,
> p. 183, emphasis added).

Next come some vignettes which require more research, some of
which the author is currently undertaking. These involve the
question: what did Christian Endeavor do, and what reading was
involved in that? And a good starting place is with the "Official
Edition" of *Christian Endeavor in All Lands*, written by the Rev.
Francis E. Clark, D.D., LL.D., the Founder of the Christian
Endeavor Movement.

The Reverend Clark wrote:

> The roots of the Christian Endeavor tree, wherever it grows,
> are Confession of Christ, Service for Christ, Fellowship with
> Christ's people, and Loyalty to Christ's Church. The farther
> I travel, the more I see of societies in every land, the more I
> am convinced that these four principles are the essential and
> the only essential principles of the Christian Endeavor
> Society. Let me repeat them:—I. Confession of Christ. II.
> Service for Christ. III. Fellowship with Christ's people. IV.
> Loyalty to Christ's Church (p. 93).

In connection with the first principle—Confession of Christ—Clark
wrote:

> I. *Confession of Christ* is absolutely necessary in the Christian
> Endeavor Society. . . . . Every week comes the prayer-

meeting, in which every member who fulfills his vow must take some part. . . . This participation is simply the confession of Christ. The true Christian Endeavorer does not take part to exhibit his rhetoric, or to gain practice in public speaking, or to show what a logical prayer he can offer to God; but he does take part to show that he is a Christian, to confess his love for the Lord. . . . The covenant pledge is simply a tried and proved device to secure frequent confession of Christ. . . . It also secures familiarity with the Word of God by promoting Bible-reading and study in preparation for every meeting. . . . Our form of confession is the prayer-meeting (*Christian Endeavor in All Lands*, pp. 94, 96).

Clark also quoted the Rev. F. B. Meyer, who not only had a substantial influence on the Oxford Group and on early A.A. ideas, but was president of the British Christian Endeavor Union. Clark quoted F. B. Meyer as follows:

Christian Endeavor stands for five great principles: (1) Personal devotion to the divine Lord and Saviour, Jesus Christ. . . . (2) The covenant obligation embodied in our pledge. . . . (3) Constant religious training for all kinds of service. . . . (4) Strenuous loyalty to the local church and denomination with which each society is connected. (5) Interdenominational spiritual fellowship (*Christian Endeavor in All Lands*, pp. 101-102).

A simple form of the much-mentioned "covenant," said Clark, was this:

Trusting in the Lord Jesus for strength, I promise Him that I will strive to do whatever He would like to have me do; that I will pray and read the Bible every day; and that, just so far as I know how, I will endeavor to lead a Christian life. I will be present at every meeting of the society, unless prevented by some reason which I can conscientiously give to my Saviour, and will take part in the meeting, either by prayer, testimony, or a Bible verse. As an active member of this

society I promise to be faithful to my own church, and to do
all I can to uphold its works and membership (*Christian
Endeavor in All Lands*, p. 252).

According to Clark, "Every Endeavor meeting has its topic, with
many Scripture references and abundant helps" (*Christian
Endeavor in All Lands*, p. 261). Clark mentioned and
recommended a Christian Endeavor text-book written by Amos R.
Wells, Editorial Secretary of the United Society of Christian
Endeavor.

The book by Wells was titled: *Expert Endeavor: A Text-book
of Christian Endeavor Methods and Principles*. Here are some of
the things it had to say about "the prayer meeting":

**What are the results that we may gain from the prayer
meeting?** They are five: original thought on religious
subjects; open committal to the cause of Christ; the helpful
expression of Christian thought and experience; the cultivation
of the spirit of worship through public prayer and through
singing; the guidance of others along all these lines of service
and life (p. 9).

**How can we get original thought on the prayer-meeting
topics?** Only by study of the Bible, followed by meditation
and observation. First, the Endeavorer should read the Bible
passage; then he should read some good commentary upon it;
then he should take the subject with him into his daily life for
five or six days, thinking about it in his odd minutes and
watching for experiences in his own life or the lives of others,
or observing nature and looking for illustrations on the subject
from all these sources (pp. 9-10).

**Are we to read Bible verses and other quotations?** Yes, all
we please, if we will make them the original expression of
our own lives by thinking about them, and adding to them
something, if only a sentence, to show that we have made
them our own. Always give the writer's name, or the part of

the Bible from which you quote. Commit the quotation to memory and do not read it (p. 11).

The author has taken the time to quote these Christian Endeavor matters because they provide real insight into the frequent comments in A.A.'s *DR. BOB and the Good Oldtimers* about Dr. Bob's intensive study of the Bible, his ability to quote Scripture freely, his using Scripture to explain questions about the A.A. program, his emphasis on and practice of prayer three times a day, his stress on outside reading of Christian literature, the prayer and meditation at early A.A. meetings, the use of outside literature and devotionals, and Dr. Bob's own very clear and continued allegiance to Jesus Christ and to Christian Fellowship throughout his days.

Because of various legends in A. A. and even some of Dr. Bob's own comments about church, many do not know the extent of Dr. Bob's commitment to God, to Jesus Christ, to the Bible, and to church life. Whatever aversion to actual church-going Dr. Bob may or may not have had—drunk or sober—the following facts are without dispute: (1) Dr. Bob was, as a youth, very much involved in the North Congregational Church in St. Johnsbury, Vermont. He was very much involved in Christian Endeavor, and the consequent prayer, Bible study, and Christian fellowship meetings. According to his son, Dr. Bob's parents were "pillars of that church" [the St. Johnsbury Congregational church]. (2) Dr. Bob belonged to St. Luke's Episcopal Church in Akron, Ohio [This information provided to the author by Dr. Bob's son]. (3) According to the records at Westminster United Presbyterian Church in Akron, Ohio, Dr. Bob and his wife Anne were charter members of that Presbyterian Church from June 3, 1936, to April 3, 1942. (4) According to the records at St. Paul's Protestant Episcopal Church in Akron, Dr. Bob became a communicant at that church about a year before he died. (5) As his son, Robert, put it, "After he sobered up, Dad [Dr. Bob] took Susie and me around to different churches. We went to the Jewish synagogue and to the Catholic church and to all of the Protestant denominations and even heard the Bible as interpreted by Mary Baker Eddy" [*Children of the Healer*, p. 127). 127].

In his tribute to Dr. Bob in the *A.A. Grapevine*, at the time of Dr. Bob's death in 1951, Bill wrote of Dr. Bob's early years in the Oxford Group after 1933:

> Anne became deeply interested in the group and her interest sustained Dr. Bob's. He delved into religious philosophy, he read the Scriptures, he studied spiritual interpretations, the lives of the Saints. Like a sponge he soaked up the spiritual philosophies of the ages.

In his book, *Not-God: The History of Alcoholics Anonymous*, Dr. Ernest Kurtz wrote:

> Bill Wilson found himself in awe of Dr. Bob's 'spiritual knowledge' and cherished the guidance of Anne Smith as each morning her pleasant voice read and interpreted the Christian Scriptures and the Oxford Group devotional books.

In our research for *Dr. Bob's Library*, we learned from Dr. Bob's daughter, Sue Smith Windows, that Dr. Bob had read all of the books mentioned in Anne Smith's spiritual journal and had an immense library of books, some then in Sue's possession, some in the possession of her brother, Robert, and some elsewhere. The author has personally inspected many of these books; and many bear, in Dr. Bob's own handwriting, the name of Dr. R. H. Smith, with the date he acquired the book, and his notation, "Please return." Sue Windows, Clarence Snyder, and many other oldtimers confirmed that Dr. Bob read, recommended, and circulated to others many of the books that he read.

In this title, we will merely list those books of a spiritual nature which we have thus far determined were a part of Dr.

Bob's reading and recommended books. A more detailed discussion will be found in Dick B., *Dr. Bob's Library*.

The following is a list by category of the spiritual books that Dr. Bob read. Some additional books that Dr. Bob read in the religious field, not pertinent to the specific categories, are listed under miscellaneous:

1.  The Bible.

2.  Books on Jesus Christ.

    George A. Barton, *Jesus of Nazareth: A Biography* (New York: The Macmillan Company, 1922).
    Harry Emerson Fosdick, *The Man from Nazareth* (Harper & Brothers, 1949).
    Harry Emerson Fosdick, *The Manhood of the Master* (London: Student Christian Movement, 1924).
    T. R. Glover, *The Jesus of History* (New York: Association Press, 1930).
    Charles Whitney Silkey, *Jesus and Our Generation* (Chicago: University of Chicago Press, 1925).
    Robert E. Speer, *Studies of the Man Christ Jesus* (New York: Fleming H. Revell, 1896).
    James Stalker, *Life of Christ*, new & rev. ed. (New York: Fleming H. Revell, 1891).

3.  Christian classics.

    *The Confessions of St. Augustine*, Translated by E. B. Pusey. A Cardinal ed. (New York: Pocket Books, 1952).
    Thomas à Kempis, *The Imitation of Christ*. A New Reading of 1441 Latin Autograph Manuscript, by William C. Creasy. (Georgia: Mercer University Press, 1989).
    Brother Lawrence, *The Practice of the Presence of God* (Pennsylvania: Whitaker House, 1982).

4. Bible devotionals.

> Oswald Chambers, *My Utmost for His Highest* (London: Simpkin Marshall, Ltd., 1927).
> Glenn Clark, *I Will Lift Up Mine Eyes* (New York: Harper & Brothers, 1937).
> Lewis L. Dunnington, *Handles of Power* (New York: Abingdon-Cokesbury Press, 1942).
> Harry Emerson Fosdick, *The Meaning of Prayer* (New York: Association Press, 1915).
> Nora Smith Holm, *The Runner's Bible* (New York: Houghton Mifflin Company, 1915).
> E. Stanley Jones, *Victorious Living* (New York, The Abingdon Press, 1936).
> E. Stanley Jones, *Abundant Living* (New York: Abingdon-Cokesbury Press, 1942).
> *The Upper Room: Daily Devotions for Family and Individual Use.* Quarterly. Grover Carlton Emmons, Editor (Nashville: General Committee on Evangelism through the Department of Home Missions, Evangelism, Hospitals, Board of Missions, Methodist Episcopal Church, South).
> Mary W. Tileston, *Daily Strength for Daily Needs* (Boston: Roberts Brothers, 1893).

5. Books on Prayer.

> Glenn Clark, *How to Find Health through Prayer* (New York: Harper & Brothers, 1940).
> Glenn Clark, *The Lord's Prayer and Other Talks on Prayer from Camps Farthest Out* (St. Paul: Macalester Park Publishing Co., 1932).
> Glenn Clark, *The Soul's Sincere Desire* (Boston: Little, Brown and Company, 1925).
> Starr Daily, *Recovery* (St. Paul: Macalester Park Publishing Company, 1948).

Mary Baker Eddy, *Science and Health with Key to the Scriptures* (Boston: Published by the Trustees under the Will of Mary Baker G. Eddy, 1916).

Charles and Cora Fillmore, *Teach Us to Pray* (Lee's Summit, MO: Unity School of Christianity, 1950).

Emmet Fox, *Getting Results by Prayer* (1933).

Emmet Fox, *The Sermon on the Mount* (New York: Harper & Row, 1934).

Gerald Heard, *A Preface to Prayer* (New York: Harper & Brothers, 1944).

Frank Laubach, *Prayer (Mightiest Force in the World)* (New York: Fleming H. Revell, 1946).

Charles M. Layman, *A Primer of Prayer* (Nashville: Tidings, 1949).

J. Rufus Mosely, *Perfect Everything* (St. Paul: Macalester Park Publishing Company, 1949).

Dr. William R. Parker and Elaine St. Johns, *Prayer Can Change Your Life*. New ed. (New York: Prentice Hall Press, 1957).

F. L. Rawson, *The Nature of True Prayer* (Chicago: The Marlowe Company, n.d.).

6. Books on Healing.

Mary Baker Eddy, *Science and Health with Key to the Scriptures* (See Prayer, above).

Charles Fillmore, *Christian Healing* (Kansas City: Unity School of Christianity, 1936).

James Moore Hickson, *Heal the Sick* (London: Methuen & Co., 1925).

Ethel R. Willitts, *Healing in Jesus' Name* (Chicago: Ethel R. Willitts Evangelists, 1931).

7.  Books on the Sermon on the Mount.

    Oswald Chambers, *Studies in the Sermon on the Mount*
      (London: Simpkin, Marshall, Ltd., n.d.).
    Emmet Fox, *The Sermon on the Mount* (See Prayer, above).
    E. Stanley Jones, *The Christ of the Mount: A Working
      Philosophy of Life* (New York: The Abingdon Press,
      1931).
    Glenn Clark, *The Soul's Sincere Desire* (See Prayer, above).
    Glenn Clark, *I Will Lift Up Mine Eyes* (See Bible devotionals,
      above).

8.  Books on Christian Love.

    Toyohiko Kagawa, *Love: The Law of Life* (Philadelphia: The
      John C. Winston Company, 1929).
    Henry Drummond, *The Greatest Thing in the World* (New
      York: Grosset & Dunlap, n.d.).
    Glenn Clark, *The Soul's Sincere Desire* (See Prayer, above).

9.  Oxford Group Books.

    (The books here listed do not include those of the Rev. Sam
    Shoemaker, which are listed immediately below. Other
    Oxford Group books which may have been read by Dr. Bob
    are listed in Chapter 7 below).

    Geoffrey Allen, *He That Cometh* (New York: The Macmillan
      Company, 1933).
    Harold Begbie, *Life Changers* (London: Mills & Boon, Ltd,
      1932).
    Amelia S. Reynolds, *New Lives for Old* (New York: Fleming
      H. Revell, 1929).
    A. J. Russell, *For Sinners Only* (London: Hodder &
      Stoughton, 1932).

A. J. Russell, *One Thing I Know* (New York: Harper & Brothers, 1933).

The Layman with a Notebook, *What Is The Oxford Group?* (London: Oxford University Press, 1933).

Howard A. Walter, *Soul Surgery: Some Incisive Thoughts on Personal Work*. 6th ed. (London: The Oxford Group, 1928).

10.  Sam Shoemaker Writings.

(It is probable that Dr. Bob read all the Shoemaker books published prior to 1940. Other Shoemaker books are listed in Chapter 8 below).

*Children of the Second Birth* (New York: Fleming Revell, 1927).

*Confident Faith* (New York: Fleming Revell, 1932).

*If I Be Lifted Up* (New York: Fleming Revell, 1931).

*The Conversion of the Church* (New York: Fleming Revell, 1932).

*Twice-Born Ministers* (New York: Fleming Revell, 1929).

*Three Levels of Life* (Pamphlet republished in *Confident Faith*).

*What If I Had But One Sermon to Preach?* (Pamphlet republished in *Religion That Works*).

11.  Books by A.A.'s "Founders."

William James, *The Varieties of Religious Experience* (New York: Vintage Books/The Library of America, 1990).

Dr. Carl G. Jung, *Modern Man in Search of a Soul* (New York: Harcourt Brace Jovanovich, 1933).

12. Books by Christian writers popular in the 1930's.

James Allen, *As a Man Thinketh* (New York: Peter Pauper Press, n.d.).

James Allen, *Heavenly Life* (New York: Grossett & Dunlap, n.d.).

Glenn Clark, *The Soul's Sincere Desire* (See Prayer, above).

Glenn Clark, *Fishers of Men* (Boston: Little Brown, 1928).

Glenn Clark, *I Will Lift Up Mine Eyes* (See Sermon, above).

Glenn Clark, *Two or Three Gathered Together* (New York: Harper & Brothers, 1942).

Glenn Clark, *How to Find Health through Prayer* (See Prayer, above).

Glenn Clark, *The Man Who Talks with Flowers* (Minn.: Macalester Park Publishing Company, 1939).

Glenn Clark, *The Lord's Prayer* (See Prayer, above).

Glenn Clark, *God's Reach* (Minn.: Macalester Park, 1951).

Glenn Clark, *Clear Horizons*. Vol. 2. Quarterly (Minn.:Macalester Park, 1941).

Glenn Clark, *Touchdowns for the Lord* (MN: Macalester Park, 1947).

Lloyd Douglas (mostly fictional; see *Dr. Bob's Library*, p. 60 for a list).

Henry Drummond, *The Greatest Thing in the World* (See Love, above).

Henry Drummond, *Natural Law in the Spiritual World* (New York: John B. Alden, 1887).

Mary Baker Eddy, *Science and Health* (See Prayer, above).

Charles Fillmore, *Christian Healing* (See Healing, above).

Charles Fillmore, *Teach Us to Pray* (See Prayer, above).

Harry Emerson Fosdick, *The Meaning of Service* (London: Student Christian Movement, 1921).

Harry Emerson Fosdick, *The Meaning of Prayer* (See Prayer, above).

Harry Emerson Fosdick, *The Manhood of the Master* (See Jesus Christ, above).

Harry Emerson Fosdick, *As I See Religion* (New York: Grossett & Dunlap, 1932).

Harry Emerson Fosdick, *On Being a Real Person* (New York: Harper & Brothers, 1943).

Harry Emerson Fosdick, *A Great Time to be Alive* (New York: Harper & Brothers, 1944).

Harry Emerson Fosdick, *The Man From Nazareth* (See Jesus Christ, above).

Emmet Fox, *The Sermon on the Mount* (See Sermon, above).

Emmet Fox, *Find and Use Your Inner Power* (New York: Harper & Brothers, 1937).

Emmet Fox, *Power Through Constructive Thinking* (New York: Harper & Brothers, 1932).

Emmet Fox, *Sparks of Truth* (New York: Grossett & Dunlap, 1941).

Emmet Fox, *Alter Your Life* (New York: Harper & Brothers, 1950).

Emmet Fox pamphlets:

*Getting Results by Prayer* (1933).

*The Great Adventure* (1937).

*You Must Be Born Again* (1936).

*Your Heart's Desire* (1937).

E. Stanley Jones, *The Christ of the Indian Road* (New York: Abingdon Press, 1925).

E. Stanley Jones, *The Christ of the Mount* (See Sermon, above).

E. Stanley Jones, *Along the Indian Road* (New York: Abingdon Press, 1939).

E. Stanley Jones, *Victorious Living* (See Bible devotionals, above).

E. Stanley Jones, *Abundant Living* (See Bible devotionals, above).

E. Stanley Jones, *Christ at the Round Table* (New York: The Abingdon Press, 1928).

E. Stanley Jones, *The Christ of Every Road* (New York: The Abingdon Press, 1930).

E. Stanley Jones, *Christ and Human Suffering* (New York: The Abingdon Press, 1933).

E. Stanley Jones, *The Choice Before Us* (New York: The Abingdon Press, 1937).

E. Stanley Jones, *The Christ of the American Road* (New York: Abingdon-Cokesbury Press, 1944).

E. Stanley Jones, *Way to Power & Poise* (New York: The Abingdon Press, 1949).

Toyohiko Kagawa, Love: *The Law of Life* (See Love, above).

Fulton Oursler (mostly fictional; See *Dr. Bob's Library*, pp. 72-73, for a list).

Norman Vincent Peale, *The Art of Living* (New York: The Abingdon Press, 1937).

Vincent Sheean, *Lead Kindly Light* (New York: Random House, 1949).

Fulton J. Sheen, *Peace of Soul* (New York: McGraw Hill, 1949).

Charles M. Sheldon, *In His Steps* (Nashville: Broadman Press, 1935).

R. Llewelyn Williams, *God's Great Plan, a Guide to the Bible* (Hoverhill Destiny Publishers, n.d.).

13.   Books on Religion and the Mind.

William James, *The Varieties of Religious Experience* (See Founders, above).

Dr. Carl G. Jung, *Modern Man in Search of a Soul* (See Founders, above).

Joshua Loth Liebman, *Peace of Mind* (New York: Simon & Schuster, 1946).

Ernest M. Ligon, *Psychology of a Christian Personality* (New York: Macmillan, 1935).

Dr. Henry C. Link, *The Rediscovery of Man* (New York: Macmillan, 1939).

Dilworth Lupton, *Religion Says You Can* (Boston: The Beacon Press, 1938).

Ralph Waldo Trine, *In Tune with the Infinite* (New York: Thomas Y. Crowell, 1897).

Ralph Waldo Trine, *The Man Who Knew* (New York: Bobbs Merrill, 1936).

14. Books about the Bible and the Church Fathers.

R. Llewlyn Williams, *God's Great Plan, A Guide to the Bible*. (See Christian writers, above).

*The Fathers of the Church* (New York: CIMA Publishing, 1947).

15. Books by modern Roman Catholic authors.

Fulton J. Sheen, *Peace of Soul* (See Christian writers, above).

16. Books about Quiet Time.

S. D. Gordon, *The Quiet Time* (London: Fleming, n.d.).

17. Miscellaneous.

Miles Menander Dawson, *The Basic Thoughts of Confucius* (New York: Garden City Publishing, 1939).

Miles Menander Dawson, *The Basic Teachings of Confucius* (Brandon Publishing Co., n.d.).

Ivan Cooke, *Kingdom Come* (London: Wright & Brown Furnell, n.d.).

Louise B. Brownell, *Life Abundant for You* (Aquarian Ministry, 1928).

Maurice Barbanelle, *Parish the Healer* (London: Ebenezer Baylis, 1941).

J. R. Moseley, *Perfect Everything* (Minn: Macalester, n.d.).

Eva B. Werber, *Quiet Talks with the Master* (Marina Del Rey, California, DeVorss, 1936).

Stewart Edward White, *Rose Dawn* (Doubleday Page, 1920).

Stewart Edward White, *Sign at Six* (New York: Bobbs Merrill, 1912).

Henry Gheon, *The Secrets of the Saints* (New York: Longman's Green, 1929).

*Teachings of the Temple* (Temple of the People Publishing, 1925).

Peter Uspenskii, *Tertium Organum* (New York: A.A. Knopf, 1922).

*The Initiate* by his Pupil (London: George Rontledge, 1944).

Alfred Noyes, *The Unknown God* (New York: Sheed & Ward, 1940).

For other "Miscellaneous" books Dr. Bob read, see Dick B., *Dr. Bob's Library*, pp. 72-80. For books more recently discovered and which may have been read by Dr. Bob, see *Dr. Bob's Library*.

# 3

# Anne Smith's Journal, 1933-1939

Dr. Bob's wife, Anne Ripley Smith, joined the Oxford Group immediately after its 30 member "team" came to Akron, Ohio, in January of 1933 at the behest of Harvey Firestone, Sr.

In company with Henrietta Seiberling, Clarace Williams, and Delphine Weber, Anne began attending Oxford Group meetings. Shortly Dr. Bob joined them and also started regularly attending.

As we mention in subsequent chapters, Henrietta Seiberling was a spearhead in the Oxford Group meetings involving Dr. Bob, Anne, T. Henry, and Clarace Williams; and Henrietta read all the Oxford Group literature of the 1930's and a good many other books as well. When the meetings involving the "alcoholic squad of the Oxford Group," and which Anne attended, were held at T. Henry's home, there were tables in T. Henry's basement furnace room containing Oxford Group literature which was made available to people attending the meetings. Anne Smith, therefore, had access to a good deal of information about Oxford Group books. Also, we recently learned that an additional Oxford Group team visited Akron in early 1934, as a follow-up on the 1933 witnessing events. Hence there was ample opportunity for Anne and Dr. Bob to learn of Oxford Group materials that were then in circulation.

Anne began, in 1933, recording in writing what she was hearing at Oxford Group meetings and what she was studying in the Bible and Christian literature. She discussed a number of the Oxford Group principles which later were to become at part of the A.A. program. Anne organized her ideas, had most of them typed up for her by her daughter, Sue Smith Windows, and assembled them in 64 pages of what we have called "Anne Smith's Journal." For further details, the reader is invited to read our title, Dick B., *Anne Smith's Journal, 1933-1939: A.A.'s Principles of Success* (San Rafael, CA: Paradise Research Publications, 1994).

The important thing here is that Anne actually read to and taught alcoholics and their families from her spiritual journal. When alcoholics and their wives would come to the home of Dr. Bob and Anne at 855 Ardmore in Akron for what was jokingly called "spiritual pablum," Anne obtained ideas for discussion from and then actually taught those present from the pages of her journal.

At six different places in her journal, Anne spoke about books she had read and was recommending. She devoted four entire pages to Toyohiko Kagawa's *Love: The Law of Life.* She quoted the well-known Christian writer, E. Stanley Jones. And she discussed a little book, written quite early in his career, by the Reverend Sam Shoemaker. It is titled *One Boy's Influence* and contains ideas which are extant in A.A. today.

Anne was very clear when it came to recommending priorities for reading. She said, "First, the Bible."

Then she suggested the following "Biographies, or stories of changed lives [that] are very helpful for the young Christian.":

Harold Begbie, *Life Changers* (London: Mills & Boon, Ltd., 1932).

Samuel M. Shoemaker, Jr., *Children of the Second Birth* (New York: Fleming H. Revell, 1927).

Amelia S. Reynolds, *New Lives for Old* (New York: Fleming H. Revell, 1929).

A. J. Russell, *For Sinners Only* (London: Hodder & Stoughton, 1932).

Harold Begbie, *Twice-Born Men* (New York: Fleming H. Revell, 1909).

Samuel M. Shoemaker, Jr., *Twice-Born Ministers* (New York: Fleming H. Revell, 1929).

She recommended books by some of the leading Christian writers of the day:

Geoffrey Allen, *He That Cometh* (New York: The Macmillan Company, 1933). Allen was an Oxford Group writer.

Samuel M. Shoemaker, Jr., *The Conversion of the Church*, (New York: Fleming H. Revell, 1932).

*All* of the E. Stanley Jones books. (We have listed the E. Stanley Jones books in Chapter 2.)

Harry Emerson Fosdick, *The Meaning of Prayer* (New York: Association Press, 1926).

Harry Emerson Fosdick, *The Manhood of the Master* (London: Student Christian Movement, 1924).

Next, she recommended reading at least one book a year on the life of Jesus Christ and specifically said of the following, "All are good.":

Rev. James Stalker, *The Life of Jesus Christ* (New York: Fleming H. Revell, 1931).

George A. Barton, *Jesus of Nazareth: A Biography* (New York: The Macmillan Company).

T. R. Glover, *The Jesus of History* (New York: Association Press, 1919).

Robert E. Speer, *Studies of the Man Christ Jesus* (New York: Fleming H. Revell, 1896).

Anne gave special attention to these books:

Toyohiko Kagawa, *Love: The Law of Life* (Philadelphia: The John C. Winston Company, 1929).

Samuel M. Shoemaker, Jr., *If I Be Lifted Up* (New York: Fleming H. Revell, 1931).

Samuel M. Shoemaker, Jr., *One Boy's Influence* (New York: Association Press, 1925).

Sue Smith Windows confirmed to the author that her father, Dr. Bob, had read all the foregoing books recommended and discussed by Anne Smith in her spiritual journal.

# 4

## *The Upper Room* and Bible Devotionals

Person after person in the annals of early A.A. mentions the
prevalence of the Bible devotionals at meetings and in the homes
of the early AAs. The meditation book most mentioned is *The
Upper Room*, a Methodist Bible devotional, which was distributed
to AAs by Lucy G., the mother of Ernie G., an early Akron A.A.
Bob E., an Akron oldtimer, said that almost every A.A. home had
one of these tiny pamphlets which were quarterlies that sold for 5
cents each. Clancy U., an early AA who had been sponsored by
Dr. Bob and by the venerable Clarence S., wrote to the manager
of Dr. Bob's Home on April 4, 1988, and recalled, "I was handed
'The Upper Room' at one of my first meetings." (See Dick B.,
*The Good Book and The Big Book*, Newton ed., pp. 52-53, n. 21.)

The following are the Bible devotionals which—as the author
ascertained from A.A. Conference approved literature, interviews
with Dr. Bob's family, Henrietta Seiberling's family, and tapes
and transcripts of oldtimers—were used in early A.A. *The Upper
Room* and *My Utmost For His Highest* were read regularly by Dr.
Bob and Anne and by Bill Wilson and Lois in the early years. The
daily devotionals were:

Oswald Chambers, *My Utmost for His Highest* (London:
Simpkin Marshall, Ltd., 1927).

Glenn Clark, *I Will Lift Up Mine Eyes* (New York: Harper & Brothers, 1937).

Lewis L. Dunnington, *Handles of Power* (New York: Abingdon-Cokesbury Press, 1942).

Harry Emerson Fosdick, *The Meaning of Prayer* (New York: Association Press, 1925).

Nora Smith Holm, *The Runner's Bible* (New York: Houghton Mifflin Company, 1915).

E. Stanley Jones, *Victorious Living* (New York: The Abingdon Press, 1936).

E. Stanley Jones, *Abundant Living* (New York: Abingdon-Cokesbury Press, 1942).

*The Upper Room: Daily Devotions for Family and Individual Use.* Quarterly. Grover Carlton Emmons, Editor (Nashville: General Committee on Evangelism through the Department of Home Missions, Evangelism, Hospitals, Board of Missions, Methodist Episcopal Church, South).

Mary W. Tileston, *Daily Strength for Daily Needs* (Boston: Roberts Brothers, 1893).

In a pamphlet titled *How to Find God* by S. M. Shoemaker, Bill Wilson's teacher, the Rev. Samuel Moor Shoemaker, Jr., wrote:

> *Read before you pray.* Read the Bible systematically. You may find helpful the serial books of devotion called *Forward Day by Day*, or the *Upper Room* or E. Stanley Jones' "Abundant Living." Use any devotional book that helps you. This draws your mind towards God, and makes you ready to pray.

The author conducted a survey among Oxford Group people who were active during A.A.'s formative years or who have had information about daily meditation passed down to them by Oxford Group activists of those early A.A. years. The oldtimers have reported to the author that the following were the principal guidebooks used for meditation:

*The Guidance of God* by Eleanor Napier Forde (Newton)
*When Man Listens* by Cecil Rose
*The God Who Speaks* by Burnett Hillman Streeter
*How Do I Begin?* by Hallen Viney

Most of the Oxford Group people were in agreement that the daily meditation book most used by Oxford Group people themselves in America was *My Utmost for His Highest* by Oswald Chambers. See Dick B., *Good Morning!: Quiet Time, Morning Watch, Meditation, and Early A.A.*, 2d ed, (Kihei, HI: Paradise Research Publications, Inc., 1998), pp. 91-94.

Jim H. of Timonium, Maryland, perhaps stands alone today as a direct source of information as to the meditation books and practices of early A.A. people in the Oxford Group *on the East Coast of the United States.* Jim was—in the 1930's—and is still today an Oxford Group activist. Until early 1996, he served on the board of Moral Re-Armament, the Oxford Group's successor in the United States. Most important, he attended Oxford Group meetings in Maryland which were also attended by the Rev. Sam Shoemaker and by A.A. co-founder, Bill Wilson. Jim reported that, in addition to the four guidebooks for daily meditation that are listed above, he used *The Quiet Time* by Howard Rose; *Vital Touch with God: How to Carry on Adequate Devotional Life* and *When I Awake*, both by Jack Winslow; *How to Find Reality in Your Morning Devotions* by Donald W. Carruthers (a book often recommended by Sam Shoemaker); *God Does Guide Us* by W. E. Sangster; and *What Is The Oxford Group?* by the Layman with a Notebook. As to daily meditation books, Jim H. said he used *My Utmost for His Highest*; *The Upper Room*; *The Meaning of Prayer* and *The Meaning of Faith* by Harry Emerson Fosdick; and *Victorious Living* by E. Stanley Jones.

Jim H. particularly called the author's attention to *A New Day: Daily Readings for Our Time* which was compiled by D. M. Prescott and originally published in 1957 by Blandford Press in

Great Britain. This devotional contains many Bible verses, comments by Oxford Group leaders, and phrases that were handed down from the Oxford Group people to early AAs themselves. One example was from a Chinese Proverb: "God gave a man two ears and only on mouth. Why don't we listen twice as much as we talk." A variant of this expression was often used by A.A. pioneer Clarence S. when he was teaching his sponsees about the prayer and meditation to be followed in A.A.'s Eleventh Step. Jim H. also recommended an Oxford Group pamphlet, *How to Listen to God*, which was prepared by John E. Batterson, and contains many specific suggestions for people willing to engage in an experiment to be in touch with God by listening to God.

# 5

# Henrietta Seiberling's Books

For a full discussion of Henrietta Seiberling's role in early A.A., see our title, *The Akron Genesis of Alcoholics Anonymous*. Henrietta was an ardent student of the Bible, quoted it frequently, and used it in her teaching and sharing at the meetings early AAs attended.

Scarcely known by AAs are the actual books which Henrietta read, and whose contents she often discussed. The following are those recalled by her children, all of whom attended early A.A. meetings in Akron:

Harold Begbie, *Life Changers*.
E. Stanley Jones's books. See Chapter 2 for list.
Samuel M. Shoemaker, *If I Be Lifted Up*.
A. J. Russell, *For Sinners Only*.
H. A. Walter, *Soul Surgery*.
A. J. Russell, *One Thing I Know*.
Glenn Clark, *The Soul's Sincere Desire*.
Glenn Clark, *I Will Lift Up Mine Eyes*.
Oswald Chambers, *My Utmost for His Highest*.
*The Upper Room*.
*All* the Oxford Group books of the 1930's. [For a list of O.G. books, see our Bibliography.]

Samuel M. Shoemaker, Jr., *Children of the Second Birth*.
Harry Emerson Fosdick, *The Meaning of Prayer*.
Brother Lawrence, *The Practice of the Presence of God*
Charles M. Sheldon, *In His Steps*.
Carl G. Jung, *Modern Man in Search of a Soul*.
Toyohiko Kagawa, *Love: The Law of Life*.
Leslie D. Weatherhead, *Discipleship* (New York: The Abingdon Press, 1934).
Leslie D. Weatherhead, *Psychology and Life* (New York: The Abingdon Press, 1935).

# 6

# T. Henry and Clarace Williams' Library

Though the author has investigated the issue, through various Oxford Group members who knew T. Henry and Clarace and also through T. Henry's daughter, there appears to be no substantial evidence today of the precise books which T. Henry and Clarace Williams read or had in their library. That these Oxford Group activists had most of the Oxford Group books and pamphlets of the day cannot be doubted. For a discussion of the roles of Mr. and Mrs. Williams in the founding of A.A., the reader should consult the author's *The Akron Genesis of Alcoholics Anonymous*.

However, the importance of the Williams home to the reading of early AAs should not be overlooked. The Bible was almost always read there at meetings. Bible devotionals, such as *The Upper Room* and *My Utmost for His Highest*, were read and discussed. *The Upper Room* was distributed there to members attending the meetings of the alcoholic squad of the Oxford Group. Oxford Group literature, such as Stephen Foot's *Life Began Yesterday*, was distributed at meetings. James Draper Newton, an Oxford Group activist for over seventy years, has confirmed to the author his personal knowledge that T. Henry and Clarace were very active in the Oxford Group both in Akron and in New York from the early 1930's to the end of the lives. Newton told the author that Oxford Group books were freely "swapped" by Oxford

Group adherents in those days. Dorothy Williams Culver personally confirmed to the author that the "furnace room" in the basement of T. Henry's home was adjacent to the place where A.A. meetings were usually held. She said the furnace room contained many tables on which Oxford Group literature was made available for use at the meetings of the alcoholic squad of the Oxford Group. She said those present did avail themselves of the literature on the tables.

While the Williams home cannot be cited as the source of any specific book, it can be cited as the place where Oxford Group literature most probably arrived in Akron for reading and circulation among early AAs, and the place from which it was probably most widely distributed to the early AAs. Many of the pioneers AAs were, as Dr. Bob put it, "broke." By contrast, Mr. and Mrs. Williams were, from time to time, quite well off, and very freely gave of their home and possessions to help those they knew in the Oxford Group. T. Henry was very active in the Oxford Group in Akron and also was a frequent attender at the meetings of the Oxford Group businessmen's team in New York where the Rev. Sam Shoemaker did much to inspire the attendees. And it was in New York that the Oxford Group bookroom was located at Rev. Shoemaker's Calvary House and from which most Oxford Group literature was disseminated in the United States.

# 7

# The Oxford Group Literature

We can examine the significance in early A.A. of Oxford Group literature in several ways. But before doing so, we should consider the "official" A.A. statements about the Oxford Group.

Bill Wilson wrote in *Alcoholics Anonymous Comes of Age* at page 39:

> The basic principles which the Oxford Groupers had taught were ancient and universal ones, the common property of mankind. . . . But the important thing is this: the early A.A. got its ideas of self-examination, acknowledgment of character defects, restitution for harm done, and working with others straight from the Oxford Groups and directly from Sam Shoemaker, their former leader in America, and from nowhere else.

In *The Language of the Heart*, Bill is quoted as follows at page 298:

> Where did the early AAs find the material for the remaining ten Steps? Where did we learn about moral inventory, amends for harm done, turning our wills and lives over to God? Where did we learn about meditation and prayer and all the rest of it? The spiritual substance of our remaining ten Steps

41

came straight from Dr. Bob's and my own earlier association with the Oxford Groups as they were then led in America by that Episcopal rector, Dr. Samuel Shoemaker.

The Foreword to the Third Edition of the Big Book says at page xvi:

> Though he [Bill Wilson] could not accept all the tenets of the Oxford Groups, he was convinced of the need for moral inventory, confession of personality defects, restitution to those harmed, helpfulness to others, and the necessity of belief in and dependence upon God.

Dr. Bob said:

> We [Bob and Bill] had both been associated with the *Oxford Group*, Bill in New York, for five months, and I in Akron, for two and a half years. Bill had acquired their idea of service. I had not, but *I had done an immense amount of reading they had recommended* (*The Co-Founders of Alcoholics Anonymous*, p. 7, emphasis added).

One might expect, then, to find a list of literature from which Bill W. and Dr. Bob learned these Oxford Group precepts. But none exists. So the author concluded that, in addition to Oxford Group-Shoemaker books that were listed or mentioned or found to have been read by Dr. Bob, Anne Smith, Henrietta Seiberling, and Mr. and Mrs. Williams, he should look for those books which the Oxford Group itself was disseminating in the 1930's. And several lists of such books did exist.

For example, almost every early Oxford Group pamphlet, which was disseminated by the Oxford Group in Great Britain, contained a list of other Oxford Group books and pamphlets that were then recommended. Moreover, Mrs. W. Irving Harris, widow of the Reverend W. Irving Harris—an assistant Minister at Calvary Episcopal Church in New York in the 1930's—informed the author that she was in charge of the Oxford Group's "bookroom" or "bookstore" in the basement of Calvary House, the virtual headquarters of the Oxford Group in America. She stated that the Calvary Church's parish publication, *The Calvary Evangel*, contained a list of Oxford Group literature which was stocked at Calvary House and which was disseminated in America in the 1930's from Calvary House.

The following includes a list of Oxford Group literature which was published in the March, 1939 issue of *The Calvary Evangel*, and which Mrs. Harris specified would have been the books disseminated from New York during the 1930's. We also include titles mentioned in issues of the *Evangel* at earlier points during A.A.'s formative period, and which titles the author personally observed, during his visit to the Calvary Church archives in New York, were recommended as Oxford Group reading:

Geoffrey Allen, *He That Cometh* (1933).
Harold Begbie, *Life Changers* (1927).
Philip M. Brown, *The Venture of Belief* (New York: Fleming Revell, 1935).
John Potter Cuyler, Jr., *Calvary Church in Action* (New York: Fleming H. Revell, 1934).
Donald W. Carruthers, *How to Find Reality in Your Morning Devotions* (Pennsylvania: State College, n.d.).
Sherwood S. Day, *The Principles of the Group* (The Oxford Group, n.d.).
Julian P. Thornton-Duesbury, *Sharing* (The Oxford Group, n.d.).
Stephen Foot, *Life Began Yesterday* (New York: Harper & Brothers, 1935).
L. W. Grensted, *The Person of Christ* (New York: Harper & Brothers, 1933).
Eleanor Napier Forde, *The Guidance of God* (1930).
Wilfrid Holmes-Walker, *New Enlistment* (The Oxford Group, circa, 1937).

Olive M. Jones, *Inspired Children* (New York: Harper & Brothers, 1933).

Olive M. Jones, *Inspired Youth* (New York: Harper & Brothers, 1938).

Victor C. Kitchen, *I Was a Pagan* (New York: Harper & Brothers, 1934).

Ebenezer MacMillan, *Seeking and Finding* (New York: Harper & Brothers, 1933).
(A copy of this title is presently located in Bill Wilson's library at Stepping Stones.)

Garth Lean and Martin Morris, *New Leadership* (London: William Heinemann, 1936).

Amelia S. Reynolds, *New Lives for Old* (New York: Fleming H. Revell, 1929).

Cecil Rose, *When Man Listens* (New York: Oxford University Press, 1937).

Howard J. Rose, *The Quiet Time* (New York: The Oxford Group at 61 Gramercy Park North, 1937).

A. J. Russell, *For Sinners Only* (1932).

Samuel Moor Shoemaker, Jr.
*Children of the Second Birth* (1927).
*Christ's Words from the Cross* (1933).
*Confident Faith* (1932).
*If I Be Lifted Up* (1931).
*National Awakening* (1936).
*Realizing Religion* (1921).
*Religion That Works* (1928).
*The Church Can Save the World* (1938).
*The Conversion of the Church* (1932).
*The Gospel According to You* (1934).

J. H. Smith, *Conversion*, n.d.

Burnett Hillman Streeter, *The God Who Speaks* (1936).

The Layman with a Notebook, *What Is The Oxford Group?* (1933).

Hallen Viney, *How Do I Begin?* (1937).

Howard A. Walter, *Soul Surgery* (1919).

Jack Winslow, *Church in Action* (no data available).
*Why I Believe in the Oxford Group* (1934).

The following are the Oxford Group books known to have been read by one or more of A.A.'s founders, but not included, prior to 1939, in the *Evangel* list:

Philip Leon, *The Philosophy of Courage* (1939).
Beverley Nichols, *The Fool Hath Said* (1936). (A copy of this is presently located at Stepping Stones.)
A. J. Russell, *One Thing I Know* (1933). (An A.A. oldtimer informed the author that he has a copy of this book with Anne Smith's signature in it.)

And there are many other books by Oxford Group writers or about the Oxford Group which are listed in our bibliography. In fact, in the Episcopal Church Archives in Austin, Texas, the author found a list among the Shoemaker papers of all the Oxford Group books which were in Sam Shoemaker's inventory of books at Calvary Church. The inventory is dated September 12, 1933. [See Appendix 1.] We cannot be certain which, if any, of the Oxford Group books in our Bibliography or in Shoemaker's inventory may or may not have been read by A.A. founders or early AAs.

# 8

# The Reverend Sam Shoemaker's Books and Writings

Whether Bill Wilson was being completely accurate or not, he attributed most of A.A.'s ideas to The Reverend Samuel Moor Shoemaker, Jr., rector of Calvary Episcopal Church in New York. Bill called Shoemaker the American Leader of the Oxford Group. This enabled Bill to credit the Oxford Group itself while pointing to a leader with whose name he apparently felt more comfortable than he did with the name of the Oxford Group's founder and leader, Dr. Frank N. D. Buchman.

Actually, Buchman was an American. He was an ordained Lutheran minister, and was born and raised in the State of Pennsylvania; and Sam Shoemaker's Calvary House was virtually the American Headquarters of Buchman's A First Century Christian Fellowship, known as the Oxford Group and then as Moral Re-Armament. Many of the Oxford Group writings known to have been read by early AAs—books such as *Soul Surgery*, *For Sinners Only*, *What Is The Oxford Group?*, *He That Cometh*, *The Fool Hath Said*, *I Was a Pagan*, *Life Began Yesterday*, *Life Changers*, *The Guidance of God*, *Seeking and Finding*, and *Inspired Children*—were not written by Shoemaker. In fact, several of these were written by Oxford Group people who had no significant, continuing contact with Shoemaker in New York.

But Shoemaker's influence on Bill Wilson was very substantial. See Dick B., *New Light on Alcoholism: The A.A. Legacy from Sam Shoemaker*. Shoemaker met with and worked closely with Bill Wilson from the earliest days of Bill's sobriety in 1934. Shoemaker led meetings at Calvary House that were attended by Bill and Lois Wilson. Shoemaker was a leader at Oxford Group houseparties that were attended by Bill and Lois Wilson. Shoemaker himself said he had close contact with Bill from the beginning of Bill's sobriety. And Bill frequently attributed his ideas to Shoemaker. The Reverend Garrett Stearly reported that Bill asked Sam Shoemaker to write the Twelve Steps, but Shoemaker declined—saying they should be written by an alcoholic (namely, Bill). Bill later submitted a multi-lith copy of the proposed Big Book text to Shoemaker before the Big Book was published. Moreover, many Oxford Group people in the New York area, who were close associates of Shoemaker's, also had substantial contact with Wilson. These included Charles Clapp, Jr., F. Shepard Cornell, Rowland Hazard, James Houck, Victor C. Kitchen, John Ryder, L. Parks Shipley, Sr., Hanford Twitchell, the Reverend Garrett Stearly, and the Reverend and Mrs. W. Irving Harris. In fact, Bill later wrote an article in which he attributed much influence on him by Sam Shoemaker *and* Rev. and Mrs. Harris.

So Shoemaker's writings were not only mentioned and read by A.A.'s founders in Akron. They inevitably were read by and influenced people who influenced Bill, whether Bill read the Shoemaker books or not.

Shoemaker's substantial writings before the Big Book was published were of three types: (1) Some fourteen major books written between 1921 and 1939; (2) Several significant pamphlets written during the same period; and (3) A steady flow of articles written by Shoemaker and published in his parish publication, *The Calvary Evangel*.

The fourteen major Shoemaker books were:

*Realizing Religion* (1923).
*A Young Man's View of the Ministry* (1923).
*Children of the Second Birth* (1927).
*Religion That Works* (1928).
*Twice-Born Ministers* (1929).
*If I Be Lifted Up* (1931).
*Confident Faith* (1932).
*The Conversion of the Church* (1932).
*Christ's Words from the Cross* (1933).
*The Gospel According to You* (1934).
*Calvary Church Yesterday and Today* (1936)
*National Awakening* (1936).
*The Church Can Save the World* (1938).
*God's Control* (1939).

Several of the pamphlets were:

*One Boy's Influence* (1925).
*The Breadth and Narrowness of the Gospel* (New York: Fleming Revell, 1929).
"The Way to Find God." *The Calvary Evangel*, August, 1935.
*Three Levels of Life* (The Oxford Group, prior to 1932).
*What If I Had But One Sermon to Preach?* (The Oxford Group, prior to 1928).
*God and America* (n.d.).
"A First Century Christian Fellowship" (*The Churchman*, 1928).
*My Life-Work and My Will*, pamphlet, n.d. (Episcopal Church Archives).

# 9

# Bill and Lois Wilson's Comments

The author has not yet found any remarks by Bill as to the books, other than the Bible, that he read prior to his writing of the Big Book and the Twelve Steps. We have already quoted the remarks he made when he interviewed T. Henry and Clarace Williams in 1954. At that time, Bill told Mr. and Mrs. Williams that he had learned much from the people in Akron and had never looked in the Bible prior to the time he visited in the Smith home for three months in 1935. We have also quoted his remarks in his 1944 lecture at Yale University to the effect that early AAs did very commonly read the Bible. As we point out in *New Light on Alcoholism*, Lois also mentioned the Bible and "Home Quiet Time" in her Oxford Group notes, which the author located and inspected at the Wilson home at Stepping Stones in Bedford Hills, New York.

Also, we located in Bill's library at his home at Stepping Stones the following three Oxford Group books:

Ebenezer Macmillan, *Seeking and Finding* (1933).
Beverley Nichols, *The Fool Hath Said* (1936).
Leslie D. Weatherhead, *Discipleship* (London: Student Christian Movement Press, 1934). Note, however, that Weatherhead was not actually a "member" of the Oxford

Group, but did write widely in depth about and with much sympathy for the Oxford Group's principles.

Bill's former secretary, Nell Wing, is in possession of Leslie D. Weatherhead's *Psychology and Life* (New York: Abingdon Press, 1935), which has Henrietta Seiberling's name in it, but was given to Nell by Bill.

Lois Wilson commented to Bill Pittman, author of *AA The Way It Began*, that Bill Wilson frequently read the Nichols book and that Bill and Lois had regularly read Oswald Chambers' *My Utmost for His Highest*. And during our last visit to Stepping Stones, we found a reference in Lois Wilson's Oxford Group note for July 22 that indicated she had just read *My Utmost For His Highest*.

To date, the author has found no pre-1939 Shoemaker books that seem to have belonged either to Bill Wilson or to Lois Wilson. We found none at Stepping Stones. None was in the possession of Nell Wing, Bill's former secretary, when we interviewed her at her New York apartment. And none was mentioned by Lois Wilson in any of the diaries or writings by her which we were permitted to inspect during our two research visits to the Wilson home at Stepping Stones in Bedford Hills, New York. In other words, if either Bill or Lois Wilson owned any of Sam Shoemaker's books that were written prior to 1939, the fact has not come to or been brought to our attention.

In his review of the books that Dr. Bob read, the author found Dr. Carl Jung's *Modern Man in Search of a Soul*. A.A.'s Big Book makes clear Jung's status as a "founder" of Alcoholics Anonymous, stemming from Jung's advice to Bill's friend and Oxford Group mentor, Rowland Hazard. In his biography of Bill Wilson, Robert Thomsen quoted Carl Jung's letter to Bill Wilson covering the Jung-Hazard relationship in 1930-1931. Then Bill's biographer states in *Bill W.*: "Ever since his early AA days, when

Bill had read Jung's *Modern Man in Search of a Soul* . . . " (p. 364). This brief reference to Jung's book indicates that Bill Wilson, as well as Dr. Bob, consulted Jung's well-known book first published in 1933.

# 10

## Nell Wing's Recollections

Nell Wing was Bill Wilson's second secretary. She was a friend and companion of Bill's wife Lois until Lois's death. And Nell's association with the Wilsons spanned forty-two years. She was the first archivist of A.A.

Page 192 of Bill Pittman's *AA The Way It Began* contains an appendix titled "Nell Wing's List of 'Books Early AAs Read.'" The following books are specified:

James Allen, *As a Man Thinketh.*
Lewis Browne, *This Believing World.*
Lewis Browne, *The Conversion Experience.*
Glenn Clark, *I Will Lift Up Mine Eyes.*
Glenn Clark, *This Changing World.*
Emmet Fox, *The Sermon on the Mount.*
William James, *The Varieties of Religious Experience.*
Richard Peabody, *The Common Sense of Drinking.*
A. J. Russell, *For Sinners Only.*
Thomas Troward, *The Edinburgh Lectures on Mental Science.*

When the author visited Nell Wing at her apartment in New York City, Nell found among her possessions a copy of Leslie D. Weatherhead's *Psychology and Life* (New York: Abingdon Press,

1935), which Henrietta Seiberling had inscribed and given to Bill Wilson. Weatherhead was a prominent religious writer of the period and often wrote about the Oxford Group.

# 11

## Pioneer Clarence S.

*That Amazing Grace: The Role of Clarence and Grace S. in Alcoholics Anonymous* is one of the author's most recent titles. Until the research for that title was undertaken, the author had been unable to pinpoint in the published remarks of A.A. oldtimers any *comprehensive specifics* about Bible verses that were studied or religious books that were read by early AAs. To be sure, there was information about what Dr. Bob and his wife, Anne, had read and recommended. Also, about Henrietta Seiberling, and T. Henry and Clarace Williams. Also, about other Oxford Group adherents. But a wellspring of specifics about books read by early AAs became available when the author interviewed Clarence's widow, Grace S., in December of 1995.

Clarence got sober in February of 1938. He was one of the forty A.A. pioneers. He was sponsored by Dr. Bob and studied the Bible and other literature under the able tutoring of Dr. Bob's wife, Anne. Clarence remained sober for many years in A.A. and until the date of his death. He addressed many A.A. gatherings. He furnished facts for A.A. Conference Approved literature. He was largely responsible for the immense growth in one year from one group to thirty of Alcoholics Anonymous in Cleveland, Ohio. Though not specifically naming Clarence, Bill Wilson's biographer, Robert Thomsen, pointed to the growth in Cleveland under Clarence's leadership, stating in *Bill W.* at page 321:

> The phenomenal growth of groups in the Cleveland area was unlike the development of A.A. anywhere else in the country. With the publication of the *Plain Dealer* articles back in '39, there'd been a veritable cloudburst of drunks in Cleveland, and ever since, new alkies had continued to pour into their meetings. They'd done a remarkable job and had solved many problems in ways that would in time become models for other groups.

For our purposes here, the reader should remember Clarence's early standing in A.A., the important role he played in A.A.'s growth, his long-term sobriety, and the fact that he passed early A.A. history to A.A. itself, to the thousands he sponsored, and to his willing student and beloved wife, Grace S.

In answer to the author's question whether Clarence said anything about the books Dr. Bob read, Grace said:

> Yes. Dr. Bob often loaned Clarence books that he [Dr. Bob] read. And he was a stickler about loaning books. When Dr. Bob loaned a book, he wrote that down; and you couldn't get a second book until you returned the first. Dr. Bob often questioned Clarence about what he had read. Doc wanted to be sure that it wasn't a drunk conning him into loaning books but not reading them. Dr. Bob wanted to be sure that Clarence was actually reading them. (Dick B., *That Amazing Grace*, p. 31).

Clarence's wife Grace specifically recalled for the author that Clarence had read and studied the following books recommended by Dr. Bob:

Harold Begbie's *Twice-Born Men*;
Brother Lawrence's *Practicing the Presence of God*;

Oswald Chambers' *My Utmost for His Highest*;

Glenn Clark's *I Will Lift Up Mine Eyes* and *Fishers of Men*;

Harry Emerson Fosdick's three books—*The Meaning of Prayer*, *The Meaning of Faith*, and *The Meaning of Service*;

William James' *The Varieties of Religious Experience*;

Toyohiko Kagawa's *Love: The Law of Life*;

Thomas a Kempis's *The Imitation of Christ*;

Victor Kitchen's *I Was a Pagan*;

A. J. Russell's *For Sinners Only*;

Samuel Shoemaker's *Children of the Second Birth* and *Twice-Born Ministers*;

St. Augustine's *Confessions*;

*The Upper Room*;

Howard A. Walter's *Soul Surgery*; and

Leslie D. Weatherhead's *Discipleship*

The foregoing list provides a treasure trove of information about what the pioneers actually read. As always, Bill spoke in generalities. Dr. Bob wrote virtually nothing about the books. Anne Smith only named a few. Consequently the list of books Clarence S. was advised to read and study shows convincingly what Dr. Bob and Anne recommended, some specifics about the pioneers' reading, and the variety of spiritual sources underlying A.A. ideas. The foregoing titles corroborate the Bible source, the Oxford Group source, the Shoemaker source, the Quiet Time source, the Anne Smith materials, and the prevalence of general Christian literature among the members of the Alcoholic Squad of the Oxford Group in Akron.

Several of Clarence's sponsees prepared two pamphlets which reflected Clarence's views on the subject of God and the subject of how to "take" the Twelve Steps of A.A. The proposed pamphlets were submitted to Clarence by these sponsees and received his approval prior to his death. They are:

*Going Through the Steps*, 2d ed. (Altamonte Springs, FL: Stephen Foreman, 1985).

*My Higher Power—The Lightbulb*, 2d ed. (Altamonte Springs, FL: Stephen Foreman, 1985).

# 12

# Comments of Other A.A. Oldtimers

We cannot here cover all the recollections of A.A. oldtimers as to their reading. Many of those recollections were not recorded, not reported, not preserved, or simply not available to the author in his research to this date.

But there are some memories which give the flavor of what was popular and what was being read for spiritual growth by the early AAs.

Possibly the most frequently mentioned piece of literature was *The Upper Room*. Dr. Bob's family, Henrietta Seiberling's family, many Akron Oldtimers, and considerable A.A. Conference approved literature all mention the wide use of *The Upper Room* at early meetings, in the homes of AAs, and in Quiet Time reading. In the same category was Chambers' *My Utmost For His Highest*—read by the Smiths and the Wilsons, and favored by Henrietta Seiberling as a daily Bible devotional. Dr. Bob used and recommended *The Runner's Bible*; and it is mentioned in the A.A. *Grapevine*'s memorial issue, published at the time of Bob's death.

Books most frequently mentioned by oldtimers were James Allen's *As A Man Thinketh*, Lewis Browne's *This Believing World*, Glenn Clark's *I Will Lift Up Mine Eyes* and *The Soul's Sincere*

*Desire*, Henry Drummond's *The Greatest Thing in the World*, Stephen Foot's *Life Began Yesterday*, Emmet Fox's *The Sermon on the Mount*, Toyohiko Kagawa's *Love. The Law of Life*, William James's *The Varieties of Religious Experience*, and A. J. Russell's *For Sinners Only*.

Books which the author found to be most in evidence as he researched archives, interviewed families of the founders, and reviewed tapes and transcripts of oldtimers were: The King James Version of the Holy Bible, Russell's *For Sinners Only*, *What Is The Oxford Group?*, Walter's *Soul-Surgery*, Allen's *As A Man Thinketh*, Begbie's *Life Changers* and *Twice-Born Men*, Chambers' *My Utmost for His Highest*, Clark's *I Will Lift Up Mine Eyes* and *The Soul's Sincere Desire*, Drummond's *The Greatest Thing in the World*, Fox's *The Sermon on the Mount*, James's *The Varieties of Religious Experience*, books by E. Stanley Jones, and *The Upper Room*.

There are a number of pamphlets which have been published either by early AAs or by local A.A. offices such as those located in Akron, Chicago, and Cleveland. Some of these pamphlets were actually commissioned by Dr. Bob, and others contained remarks by oldtimers that are indicative of what they had learned and passed on from very early years. These pamphlets are:

> *A Manual for Alcoholics Anonymous* (Akron, Ohio: AA of Akron).
> *A Guide to the Twelve Steps of Alcoholics Anonymous* (Akron, Ohio: AA of Akron).
> *Spiritual Milestones in Alcoholics Anonymous* (Akron, Ohio: AA of Akron).
> *Second Reader for Alcoholics Anonymous* (Akron, Ohio: AA of Akron).
> *AA: God's Instrument* (Chicago: Chicago Area Alcoholics Anonymous Service Office).

*"It's All in the Mind,"* (Chicago: Chicago Area Alcoholics Anonymous Service Office).

*The New Way of Life: A.A.* (Cleveland: The Cleveland District Office of Alcoholics Anonymous).

Roy L. Smith, *Emergency Rations* (Cleveland: The Cleveland District Office of Alcoholics Anonymous).

*The Four Absolutes* (Cleveland: Cleveland Central Committee of A.A.).

*Handles for Sobriety*, comp. A Member of Alcoholics Anonymous (Cleveland: The Cleveland District Office of Alcoholics Anonymous).

Clyde G., *My Quiet Time* (Cleveland: Alcoholics Anonymous).

*Handles and Hodge Podge*, comp. a member of Alcoholics Anonymous (Cleveland: The Cleveland District Office of Alcoholics Anonymous).

*A.A. Sponsorship—Its Opportunities and Its Responsibilities* (Cleveland: Cleveland Ohio District Office, n.d.)

Charles L. Wood, *Prayers for Alcoholics* (Cincinnati, Ohio: Forward Movement Publications, n.d.). From a Midwest Intergroup Office.

Edward J. Delehanty, M.D., *The Therapeutic Value of the Twelve Steps of A.A.* (Salt Lake City, Utah: Utah Alcoholism Foundation, n.d.). From a Midwest Intergroup Office.

*The Devil and A.A.* (Chicago: Chicago Area Alcoholics Anonymous Service Office, 1948).

*A Guide to Serenity* (Cleveland: The Cleveland District Office of Alcoholics Anonymous.

*Alcoholics Anonymous: An Interpretation of Our Twelve Steps* (Washington, D.C.: "The Paragon" Creative Printers, n.d.)

*Cleveland Central Bulletin* (1942 et. seq.)

# 13

# Some Suggestions for You

While there are literally hundreds of books which provide the backdrop for A.A.'s spiritual roots, there are some simple and helpful keys to your review and study. These the author discovered as he assembled the several sources of A.A.'s spiritual principles.

Before we begin, let's review the sources: (1) The Bible. (2) The meditation books that were used in connection with Quiet Time. (3) The life-changing program of the Oxford Group. (4) The teachings of Sam Shoemaker. (5) The materials in Anne Smith's Journal. (6) The religious books that Dr. Bob studied and circulated. See particularly: Dick B., *Utilizing Early A.A.'s Spiritual Roots for Recovery Today* (Kihei, HI: Paradise Research Publications, Inc., 1998).

We will not deal here with details covered comprehensively in our other titles. But we will suggest some key items to read in connection with each of A.A.'s six major spiritual sources; and we refer the reader to the particular books in our research series that can help with the background and specifics.

# The Bible

Early AAs did not skimp on the portions of the Good Book they studied. Dr. Bob read the entire Bible three times and quoted from it often. He studied it daily. Clarence S. not only read the Bible from cover to cover but strongly urged his sponsees to do likewise. Anne Smith was thoroughly conversant with Scripture. The books the pioneers read were primarily concerned with the Bible. And both of the Oxford Group leaders who influenced A.A. the most were insistent upon the importance of Bible study. Oxford Group Founder Frank Buchman was said to be "soaked in the Bible." And he had two groups of well-known expressions about how to study the Bible: The first was: Observe accurately. Interpret honestly. Apply drastically. The second was: Study it through. Write it down. Pray it in. Live it out. Sam Shoemaker, the Oxford Group's most prolific writer (and the man Bill Wilson dubbed a "co-founder" of A.A.) was known as a "Bible Christian." Shoemaker often taught that one should study and know the Bible and all else would fall into place.

It would not be appropriate in this bibliography to detail the Bible segments that were of greatest importance in early A.A. For such specifics, the reader is referred to two of our titles: *Turning Point: A History of Early A.A. 's Spiritual Roots and Successes* and *The Good Book and The Big Book: A.A. 's Roots in the Bible.*

Yet there are some biblical concepts that were central in all of A.A.'s source books.

We begin with the *biblical names for God*—Creator, Maker, Almighty God, God of our Fathers, Father, Spirit. For these biblical names from the Good Book can be found in the Twelve Steps, A.A.'s Big Book, and much of the earlier A.A. literature.

Then follow the Step concepts.

**Step One**: Mankind's state of *despair* before the need for God is discovered. See: "O wretched man that I am! who shall deliver me from the body of this death?" (Romans 7:24).

**Step Two**: Three biblical stepping stones on the path to **"finding" God**. See (1) ". . . for he that cometh to God must **believe** that he is, and *that* he is a rewarder of them that diligently seek him" (Hebrews 11:6; bold face added); (2) "If any man **will do his will**, he shall **know** of the doctrine, whether it be of God . . ." (John 7:17, bold face added); (3) "But **seek** ye first the kingdom of God . . ." (Matthew 6:33, bold face added).

**Step Three**: The *surrender*. See "Thy will be done . . ." (Matthew 6:10).

**Step Four**: *Self-examination*. See: "And why beholdest thou the mote [speck] that is in thy brother's eye, but considerest not the beam [log] that is in thine own eye?" (Matthew 7:3).

**Step Five**: *Confession*. See: "Confess *your* faults one to another. . . ." (James 5:16).

**Step Six**: *Conviction*. See: "Against thee, thee only, have I sinned, and done *this* evil in thy sight . . ." (Psalm 51:4); and "Iniquities prevail against me: as *for* our transgressions, thou shalt purge them away" (Psalm 65:3).

**Step Seven**: *Conversion*. See: ". . . Ye must be born again" (John 3:7); and "Humble yourselves in the sight of the Lord, and he shall lift you up" (James 4:10).

**Step Eight**: *Reconciliation*: See "Agree with thine adversary quickly . . ." (Matthew 5:25).

**Step Nine**: *Restitution* (amends). See: "Therefore if thou bring thy gift to the altar, and there rememberest that thy brother hath ought against thee; Leave there thy gift before the altar, and go thy way; first be reconciled to thy brother . . ." (Matthew 5:23-24).

**Step Ten**: *Daily surrender*. See: "Watch and pray, that ye enter not into temptation: the spirit indeed *is* willing, but the flesh *is* weak" (Matthew 26:41).

**Step Eleven**: There are five basic ideas underlying this important Step linking the alcoholic to God. (1) *Prayer works*. See: "The effectual fervent prayer of a righteous man availeth much" (James 5:16). (2) *Forgiveness is available*. See: "And the prayer of faith shall save the sick, and the Lord shall raise him up; and if he have committed sins, they shall be forgiven him" (James 5:15); and "If we confess our sins, he is faithful and just to forgive us *our* sins, and to cleanse us from all unrighteousness" (1 John 1:9). (3) *Divine guidance and communication are available*. See: "My voice shalt thou hear in the morning, O Lord; in the morning will I direct *my prayer* unto thee, and will look up" (Psalm 5:3); "If any of you lack wisdom, let him ask of God, that giveth to all *men* liberally, and upbraideth not; and it shall be given him" (James 1:5); and "Trust in the Lord with all thine heart; and lean not unto thine own understanding. In all thy ways acknowledge him, and he shall direct thy paths" (Proverbs 3:5-6). (4) *Spiritual growth is available*. See: "Study to shew thyself approved unto God, a workman that needeth not to be ashamed, rightly dividing the word of truth" (2 Timothy 2:15); and "Search the scriptures . . ." (John 5:39). (5) *Continual peace through trust in God is available*. See: "Thou wilt keep *him* in perfect peace, *whose* mind *is* stayed on *thee*: because he trusteth in thee" (Isaiah 26:3).

**Step Twelve**: *The result of these steps*. (1) AN AWAKENING. See: "But ye shall *receive power*, after that the Holy Ghost is come upon you: and ye shall be witnesses unto me . . ." (Acts 1:8, italics added); and "Therefore if any man *be* in Christ, *he* is a **new creature**: old things are passed away; behold, all things are become new" (2 Corinthians 5:17, bold face added). (2) A DUTY TO SHARE: *Carry the message.* See: ". . . *faith without works* is dead" (James 2:20, italics added); "Now then we are *ambassadors for Christ*, as though God did beseech you by us . . ." (2 Corinthians 5:20, italics added); and "Follow me, and I will make you *fishers of men*" (Matthew 4:19, italics added). (3) LIVING LOVE by *practicing the principles God lays down in His Word.* See the Ten Commandments. These and Jesus's Sermon on the Mount, 1 Corinthians 13, and the Book of James all contain spiritual principles AAs adopted. So do the "Four Absolutes" of the Oxford Group which are discussed below.

There were several key books early AAs were urged to study concerning the Bible. As to Matthew 5-7 (the Sermon on the Mount), there were Oswald Chambers's *Studies in the Sermon on the Mount*, Glenn Clark's *I Will Lift Up Mine Eyes* and *The Lord's Prayer and Other Talks on Prayer from The Camp Farthest Out*, Emmet Fox's *The Sermon on the Mount*, and E. Stanley Jones's *The Christ of the Mount.* As to 1 Corinthians 13 (the so-called "love chapter" and the subject of love, there were Glenn Clark's *The Soul's Sincere Desire*, Henry Drummond's *The Greatest Thing in the World and other Addresses*, and Toyohiko Kagawa's *Love: The Law of Life.* As to many of the verses in the Book of James, there was Nora Smith Holm's *The Runner's Bible.* There were several others on the life and teachings of Jesus Christ which the reader can find in our bibliography.

## The Oxford Group

The Oxford Group was founded by Dr. Frank N. D. Buchman, an ordained Lutheran Minister from Pennsylvania. Its program focused on *life-changing.* Later, the group also spoke about "world-changing through life-changing." The group was a non-denominational fellowship dedicated to bringing people to Christ in order to find God and change their lives. In the words of

Buchman: Sin was the problem. Jesus Christ was the cure. And the result was a miracle. Crucifixion of the "Big I" (Ego) was said to be necessary. And this crucifixion was accomplished, they said, by "self-surrender."

For much of the period before AAs became a part, and during the period they were part, of the Oxford Group, that group was called "A First Century Christian Fellowship." That name seemed particularly important in the American segment, and the Reverend Sam Shoemaker used it often. About the period AAs became detached from the Oxford Group (first, in New York in 1937; and then, in Akron, about 1940), the Group began using the name "Moral Re-Armament"—particularly because of the Group's focus at that juncture on attempting to bring peace through persuading individuals, then leaders, then nations, and then the world to turn to Christ and live under "a Dictatorship of the Holy Spirit," utilizing Christian precepts.

**Oxford Group Steps?**

Contrary to what a number of people have written, the Oxford Group did not have "six steps." Nor did it have some of the other "numbered" ideas which were attributed to it. One anonymous writer (who was not a member of the Oxford Group) wrote that the Group had "four points which are the keys to the kind of spiritual life God wishes us to lead." However, the Oxford Group did not refer to these four "points." They did subscribe to the "Four Absolutes," which they also called the "Four Standards," and which were derived from the teachings of Jesus. Oxford Group people were to measure their lives by these standards through self-examination and confession and also were to try to live by these standards once their lives had been changed through a spiritual experience or awakening. The Oxford Group did not have "four practical spiritual activities," which the same non-Oxford Group writer specified as: Sharing, Surrendering, Restitution, and Listening to God. One writer said the Oxford

Group was based on "seven assumptions." Another writer said it had "Eight Points."

## Key Oxford Group Principles

But the real keys were laid out by founder Dr. Frank Buchman and also taught by Bill Wilson's friend, Sam Shoemaker. The principal Oxford Group keys can probably be summarized as follows: (1) First, the "Four Absolutes"—Honesty, Purity, Unselfishness, and Love; (2) Second, the "Five C's" which embodied the Group's life-changing "art." These five were: "Confidence, Confession, Conviction, Conversion, and Conservation" (later called "Continuance"). (3) Third, Sharing for witness. (4) Fourth, Quiet Time and the guidance of God. (5) Fifth, Restitution. (6) Last, the seven biblical principles of the Group. These seven principles were written by The Reverend Sherwood Sunderlund Day (close friend of Buchman and Shoemaker), published in an Oxford Group pamphlet, and also published by Shoemaker's Calvary Church. They focused on such items as fellowship, teamwork, and loyalty.

As the result of his reading of hundreds of Oxford Group books and conferring with Oxford Group survivors, the author reconstructed some twenty-eight Oxford Group concepts that heavily influenced A.A. ideas. There are hundreds of books by and about the Oxford Group; and one can find himself in a merry chase trying to fathom the ideas relevant to A.A. That is why the author wrote several titles on the subject. There are almost two hundred Oxford Group words, phrases, and ideas that were transported directly to A.A. There are some twenty-eight Oxford Group spiritual principles which impacted upon A.A. And Oxford Group ideas can be found directly underlying each of A.A.'s Twelve Steps. Bill Wilson eventually so conceded. And this is both consistent with, and not surprising in view of, Dr. Bob's statement that A.A.'s basic ideas came from the Bible, and the Oxford Group's statement that the principles of the Oxford Group *were* the principles of the Bible. The best study the author has written on this subject is *The Oxford Group & Alcoholics Anonymous: A Design for Living That Works*. The foregoing title sets forth the twenty-eight Oxford Group ideas that influenced A.A., and which can be grouped as follows: (1) **About God**: (a) God is the Almighty God of the Bible. (b) God has a plan—His will for man. (3) Man's chief end is to do God's will. (4) You start by believing that God *is*. (2) **About sin**: It exists. Sin is defined as that which blocks man from God and from other people. And it is best described in terms of the "spiritual malady" of self-centeredness—estrangement from God in people who were meant to be His companions. (3) **Finding God**: (a) This was achieved, they said, through surrender of self—the turning point. (b) Through the technique or "art" of soul-surgery—eliminating sin, the barrier to God. And (c) the resultant life-change. (4) **The path to the relationship with God**: (The reader can readily see the relationship to the Twelve Steps.) The path involves a *decision* (Step Three); *self-examination* (Step Four); *confession* (Step Five); *conviction*-readiness to hate and forsake sin (Step Six); *conversion*—rebirth (Step Seven); and *restitution* (Steps Eight and Nine). (5) **Jesus Christ**—the vital transforming power. The Oxford Group and early A.A. certainly believed that man could not change himself, could not find God by himself, and could not pray or meditate or live a new life by himself. There had to be rebirth through turning to Christ—the way, truth, and life. (6) **Spiritual growth—continuance**: The job was not over when the rebirth occurred. Man had to continue to grow spiritually; and this was a basic precept in the Oxford Group and in *A.A.'s last three Steps*. The continuance principle involved daily surrender as a process, divine guidance, living by the Four Absolutes, Quiet Time, Bible study, prayer, listening to God, writing down the guidance received, and perhaps "checking" the thoughts against Scripture and the teachings of Jesus—and sometimes with other believers. (7) **A spiritual experience or awakening**: The result of the life-changing procedures was knowledge of God and His Will *and* "God-consciousness"—often called an "experience of God" in which His power and presence were perceived. (8) **Fellowship and**

**Witness**: "Faith without works" was a strong Oxford Group action idea. There was to be a building up by teams, groups, and fellowship with other believers. And the practice was then to pass the message on *by witness* and *by living the changed life.*

### The Oxford Group's Own Resource Literature

Several resource materials were commonly read and used in the Oxford Group of the 1930's in connection with the principles and practices of the program: (1) **On Oxford Group principles**: Sherwood Sunderland Day's *The Principles of the Group* and A. J. Russell's *For Sinners Only.* (2) **On willingness, believing, and seeking**: Philip Marshall Brown's *The Venture of Belief.* (3) **On Sharing for confession and witness**: Julian P. Thornton-Duesbury's *Sharing.* (4) **On the Five C's**: Howard Walter's *Soul Surgery.* (5) **On the Four Absolutes**: The Layman with a Notebook's *What is the Oxford Group?* (6) **On Guidance**: Eleanor Napier Forde's *The Guidance of God.* (7) **On Quiet Time**: Howard Rose's *The Quiet Time* and Jack C. Winslow's *When I Awake.* (8) **On "Listening"**: Cecil Rose's *When Man Listens.* (9) **On beginning the program**: Hallen Viney's *How Do I Begin?* (10) **And on the result**: Burnett Hillman Streeter, *The God Who Speaks.*

# Sam Shoemaker—"Co-founder" of A.A.

Bill Wilson was fond of attributing all of A.A.'s spiritual ideas to Sam Shoemaker. He erroneously called Shoemaker the "American leader" of the Oxford Group. But neither Shoemaker himself nor the Oxford Group leaders the author interviewed would acknowledge the leadership role Wilson assigned to his friend Sam. There was a conscious effort  by Wilson to avoid the prejudice against the Oxford Group by crediting Shoemaker. However, there is no denying that Shoemaker was the most prolific Oxford Group writer, its best known figure in the United States (other than Buchman), and the Oxford Group person who had the most direct impact upon the thinking and writing of Bill Wilson.

Buchman's biographer Garth Lean pointed out to the author that there was little or nothing that Shoemaker taught that could not be found in other Oxford Group writings. But the author found every Oxford Group idea beautifully expressed in Shoemaker's fourteen pre-Big Book titles. A thorough study of the Shoemaker contribution can be found in the author's *New Light on Alcoholism: The A.A. Legacy of Sam Shoemaker*. And the reader is directed to that work for the details, an analysis, and a perspective. Unfortunately, most of the important Shoemaker books of the 1920's and 1930's are not only out-of-print, but almost impossible to obtain. Nonetheless, a tremendous insight into the actual writing and thinking of Shoemaker can be obtained from the Shoemaker titles listed below.

**Shoemaker's Impact on Bill W.**

The reader should note that Shoemaker's colleague, The Reverend Garrett Stearly twice reported that Bill Wilson asked Shoemaker to write the Twelve Steps, with Shoemaker declining. Then Wilson furnished Shoemaker with a manuscript copy of the Big Book for review. And there are a number of words and phrases in A.A. literature that seem to have been taken from Shoemaker's words. The author believes the following major Shoemaker ideas impacted heavily on Wilson's thinking: (1) **Shoemaker's proposed experiment of faith**—emphasizing John 7:17 ("If any man will do his [God's] will, he shall know of the doctrine, whether it be of God, or *whether* I speak of myself."). (2) **Shoemaker's suggestions on prayer**: These emphasized "Thy will be done" from the Lord's Prayer and the expectant waiting suggested in 1 Samuel 3:9 ("Speak, Lord, thy servant heareth") and Acts 9:6 ("Lord, what wilt thou have me to do?"). (3) **Shoemaker's teachings about morning devotions**: He strongly urged a morning quiet time with Bible study, prayer, listening, journalizing, and the use of devotional books where they can be helpful. (4) **Shoemaker's advice relevant to today's A.A.**: This included the suggestion that people surrender as much of themselves as they understand to as much of God as they understand—a direct precursor of the God-as-we-understood-Him idea in the Twelve Steps. For unbelievers, Shoemaker suggested they "come to believe" by "acting as if." As for those hostile to a belief in God, Shoemaker stood his ground on the proposition that a belief in God is nonetheless essential—a position Dr. Bob took with unwavering firmness. Bob's position is clear from the last page of his story on page 181 of the Third Edition of the Big Book. Shoemaker's four major ideas are discussed at length in the author's comprehensive title: *Turning Point: A History of Early A.A.'s Spiritual Roots and Successes.*

### Shortcuts to Shoemaker

For the reader who wants a capsulized picture of Shoemaker's thoughts about A.A.—an explanation in Shoemaker's own words—there are the three articles Shoemaker wrote, regarding the Twelve Steps: (1) *12 Steps to Power*; (2) *The Twelve Steps of A.A.: What They Can Mean to the Rest of Us*; and (3) *Those Twelve Steps as I Understand Them.* There are also Shoemaker's two addresses at A.A.'s own International Conventions in 1955 and 1960. The first speech can be found in *Alcoholics Anonymous Comes of Age.* The second is summarized in and the author's *New Light on Alcoholism.* In addition, Shoemaker's daughter Nickie Shoemaker Haggart assembled some key Shoemaker ideas in a book written immediately following Shoemaker's death. This title was *Sam Shoemaker at His Best: Extraordinary Living for the Ordinary Man.* And there are several reprints of an important Shoemaker article in *The Calvary Evangel* (1935): *How to Find God.* This article is especially significant when one considers the phrase AAs read at virtually every meeting: "There is One who has all power. That One is God. May you find Him now!"

# Anne Smith's Spiritual Journal

To the author's knowledge, no significant work has been done on Anne Smith's spiritual journal (a journal kept by Dr. Bob's wife) other than the material covered in our own title, *Anne Smith's Journal, 1933-1939: A.A.'s Principles of Success*. In our view, Anne's journal is critical to an understanding of A.A.'s spiritual roots. Anne assembled, wrote, and taught from this journal from 1933 to 1939. It contains the Bible ideas, the Oxford Group principles, the Twelve Step concepts, and the literature suggestions upon which A.A. was founded.

When Bill Wilson lived with the Smiths in the summer of 1935, Anne was reading Scripture and covering other Christian literature with Bill Wilson and Anne's husband Dr. Bob. Later, Anne held Quiet Time each morning at the Smith home in Akron where Scripture reading, prayer, meditation, and the reading of literature occurred. The author is certain that Anne's journal must have figured prominently in this teaching. Also, early AAs and their families would come to the Smith home for what they jokingly called "spiritual pablum." Anne would read to them from her journal, suggest a spiritual topic for discussion, and then lead the discussion.

Valuable also were the suggestions by Anne for spiritual reading. She specified daily Bible study as number one in importance. Then she listed Oxford Group books, Shoemaker books, books by E. Stanley Jones, life-changing stories, and books on the life of Jesus Christ, as well as books on prayer and love.

# The Spiritual Literature Early AAs Read

The spiritual literature early AAs read is, of course, the subject of this Seventh Edition. However, the reader will want to obtain a copy of the author's *Dr. Bob's Library: Books for Twelve Step Growth* and *That Amazing Grace: The Role of Clarence and Grace*

*S. in Alcoholics Anonymous.* These two titles show how Dr. Bob, Anne, Henrietta, and Clarence S. used Christian literature to feed the spiritually hungry early AAs and their families. *The Akron Genesis of Alcoholics Anonymous* provides a narrative account of how it all came together at A.A.'s birthplace.

## The Daily Meditation Books of Early A.A.

Our title, *Good Morning!: Quiet Time, Morning Watch, Meditation, and Early A.A.* furnishes a complete guide as to how early A.A.'s observed Quiet Time. It details the time they set aside each morning; their quiet stance; and their Bible study, prayer, listening, writing down, checking, and use of helpful Christian literature. If the reader wishes to learn how Quiet Time can be observed today just as the highly successful early AAs did it, then this is the book to study.

The Quiet Time of early A.A. bears little resemblance to A.A. prayer and meditation today. For one thing, the pioneers insisted on belief in God. Bible study was vital. A relationship with God through Jesus Christ was part of the picture. Then there was group prayer, listening, journalizing, and checking. Meditation books and pamphlets were "helpful" and "supplemental." They certainly were not the essence of Quiet Time. They were just a guide to thinking and discussion. It was the direct contact with God (called two-way prayer) by asking and listening that was critical The four principal materials, in the order of their popularity, were *The Upper Room* (Methodist quarterly), *My Utmost for His Highest* by Oswald Chambers, *Victorious Living* by E. Stanley Jones, and *Daily Strength for Daily Needs* by Mary W. Tileston. All provide a Bible verse for reflection, Scripture references for further study, a prayer, and a thought for the day. They were not intended to replace the entirety of Quiet Time which often took an hour each day.

## Putting It All Together

As the author was completing his sixth year of research, he was asked to do a weekend seminar at The Wilson House (the birthplace of Bill Wilson and, nearby, the burial plot for Bill and Lois Wilson) at East Dorset, Vermont. The topic was the early spiritual history of A.A. The seminar took eleven hours. The talk has been taped by Glen K. Tapes and gave rise to the comprehensive history the author had published in 1997. For a comprehensive study of early A.A.'s spiritual roots and successes, this recent title contains the necessary material. It is 776 pages in length, has appendices, a bibliography, a Scripture Index, and a General Index. The title is *Turning Point: A History of Early A.A.'s Spiritual Roots and Successes.*

In May of 1998, the author moved a step closer to summarizing in concise form the six major sources of A.A.'s spiritual ideas. His ideas were presented at his third seminar at The Wilson House. They were again taped by Glenn K. Audio Tapes. And the subject matter of the seminar is covered completely in Dick B., *Utilizing Early A.A.'s Spiritual Roots for Recovery Today* (1998).

# 14

# Conclusion

Bill Wilson wrote in *As Bill Sees It*:

> We are only operating a spiritual kindergarten in which people are enabled to get over drinking and find the grace to go on living to better effect. Each man's theology has to be his own quest, his own affair (p. 95).

An Akron A.A. oldtimer, Wally G., had this to say about early efforts toward everyday spiritual growth:

> I remember the first meeting I attended was led by Dick S. He opened the meeting with a short prayer, read a passage from the Bible which I do not recall, and talked about that in its relationship to the everyday life of those present.

Another oldtimer—Earl T., who was sponsored by Dr. Bob, said:

> I remember most distinctly the first meeting that I attended—Bill D. [A.A. Number Three] sat with the Holy Bible in his lap. The meeting had been opened with a prayer. Bill read excerpts from the Bible and translated them into everyday life.

At another point, Wally G. said:

> You would be surprised at how little talk there was of
> drinking experiences. That was usually kept for interviews in
> the hospital at that time, or interviews with a prospect who
> wasn't too sure. We were more interested in our everyday life
> than we were in reminiscing about drinking experiences and
> that type of thing. Anyway we followed this *Upper Room*
> which was a quarterly publication of the Methodist Church
> South, I believe, although it was non-sectarian in character
> and consisted of a verse or story in support of the verse from
> the Bible for each day, and a thought for the day, together
> with a suggestion as to our reading.

Pioneer William V. H. said:

> This *Upper Room* was a little daily reading booklet that I've
> used ever since. It's published by the Methodist Church
> authority down in Nashville, Tennessee. At first, when there
> were quite a few in the group, each member was furnished
> with a copy which was good for three months of daily
> readings. . . . I credit my success to a lot of the daily
> readings.

The author believes that these remarks by Bill Wilson and
others demonstrate that, from its very beginnings, A.A. never
attempted to be a substitute for religion, for church, or for spiritual
reading. Bill frequently characterized A.A. as a spiritual
kindergarten. And AAs began, from the very beginning, to grow
spiritually by looking for further information in spiritual
sources—the Bible, the daily Bible devotionals, the writings of
spiritual leaders of the day, the literature by Sam Shoemaker, and
the other Oxford Group books then available. This approach was
incorporated in the Big Book, in non-denominational terms, by
suggesting that AAs make use of *outside reading* (reading in
addition to A.A.'s Conference Approved literature) and get
recommendations in that area from their rabbi, minister, or priest.

Anne Smith had previously made the same kind of recommendation in the spiritual journal she read to early AAs in Akron.

We close by referring to this verse from 2 Timothy 2:25 (King James Version):

> Study to shew thyself approved unto God, a workman that needeth not to be ashamed, rightly dividing the word of truth.

We sincerely hope this bibliography of the books that early AAs read for spiritual growth can become a vehicle for the reader to discover for himself or herself the roots of many of the spiritual words and ideas in A.A. More importantly, this list of titles should enable the reader to examine and profit from the spiritual books read by the A.A. pioneers as they sought to maintain a fit spiritual condition and grow in spiritual understanding and knowledge.

END

# Appendix
## Inventory of Books on Hand at Calvary House
## September 12, 1933 *

(List found at the Archives of
the Episcopal Church U.S.A., Austin, Texas)

*An Apostle to Youth* (old style) [John McCook Roots]
*An Apostle to Youth* [John McCook Roots]
*Guidance of God* [Eleanor Forde]
*Principles of the Group* [Sherwood S. Day]
*Sharing* [Julian P. Thornton-Duesbury]
*How to Find Reality* [Donald W. Carruthers]
*Quiet Time* [Howard Rose]
*Three Levels of Life* [Samuel Shoemaker]
*Letter #7* [1930]
*A Med. Oxford Group* *
*One Boy's Influence* [Samuel Shoemaker]
*The Church and the Oxford Groups* *
*Stories of Our Oxford Group H. P.* *
*Jesus Christ and Mental Health* *
*Groups Came to Louisville* *
*What If I Had But One Sermon to Preach* [Samuel Shoemaker]
*Meaning of Conversion* *
*It Turned out to Be a Revival* *
*For Doubters Only* *
*Group Leadership* *
*A First Century Christian Fellowship* *
*Oxford Group in Aberdeen* *

83

*Seek Ye First* *
*Atlantic Monthly*, Dec., 1928 *
*The Group Stirs Religious Life in Asheville* *
*The Student, the Fish and Agassiz* *
*The First Century Ch. Fellowship Today* *
*For Sinners Only* (American) [A. J. Russell]
*For Sinners Only* (English) [A. J. Russell]
*He That Cometh* [Geoffrey Francis Hallen]
*The Conversion of the Church* [Samuel Shoemaker]
*Life Changers* [Harold Begbie]
*Children of the Second Birth* [Samuel Shoemaker]
*Twice Born Ministers* [Samuel Shoemaker]
*Soul Surgery* [H. A. Walter]
*Realizing Religion* [Samuel Shoemaker]
*A Young Man's View of the Ministry* [Samuel Shoemaker]
*Religion That Works* [Samuel Shoemaker]
*If I Be Lifted Up* [Samuel Shoemaker]
*Confident Faith* [Samuel Shoemaker]
*Seeking and Finding* [Ebenezer Macmillan]
*For Sinners Only* (German)
*Unter Gottes Fuhrun* *
*God in the Slums* *
*God in the Shadows* *
*Moffatt N. T.*
*New Lives for Old* [Amelia S. Reynolds]
*Creative Prayer* [E. Herman]
*Time*, June 8, 1931
*Londay Daily Express*, April 16, 1932
*Akron Times Press*, January 21, 1933
Misc. Amer. newspapers--Dec. 1932-Feb. 1933
Church of Eng. newspapers misc. 1932
Church of Eng. newspapers, old files of M. Reynolds
Church of Eng. newspapers, June 3, 1932
Church of Eng. newspapers, July 8, 1932
Church of Eng. newspapers, July 15, 1932
*Sunday Referee*, July 12, 1931

Misc. English papers, 1932
*Detroit Free Press*, May 28, 1932
*Los Angeles Times*, Feb. 6-8, 1933
*Development of the Group in Average Parish*
"Things Old and New" (*Christian Observer*)
"Things in Common" (*Christian Observer*)
"Moral Content" (*Christian Observer*)
*Sunday Chronicle*, Mar. 13, 1932
The Work of Frank Buchman--one large box of papers, Detroit, KC, Louisville
Article by Russell (C. O.), Oct. 21, 1931
*First Cent. Ch. Fell.* by S. M. S., Jr.
Happy Am I
Group System in the Catholic Church
Cleve Hicks' Bible Study Lessons
    * Copies of these books have not yet been located.

# Bibliography

## Alcoholics Anonymous

*Publications About*

*Alcoholics Anonymous.* (multilith volume). New Jersey: Works Publishing Co., 1939.

*Alcoholics Anonymous: The Story of How More Than 100 Men Have Recovered from Alcoholism.* New York City: Works Publishing Company, 1939.

B., Dick. *Anne Smith's Journal, 1933-1939: A.A.'s Principles of Success.* 3rd ed. Kihei, HI: Paradise Research Publications, Inc., 1998.

———. *The Oxford Group & Alcoholics Anonymous: A Design for Living That Works.* Kihei, HI: Paradise Research Publications, 1998.

———. *Dr. Bob and His Library: A Major A.A. Spiritual Source.* 3rd ed. Kihei, HI: Paradise Research Publications, Inc. 1998.

———. *New Light on Alcoholism: The A.A. Legacy from Sam Shoemaker.* Corte Madera, CA: Good Book Publishing Company, 1994.

———. *That Amazing Grace: The Role of Clarence and Grace S. in Alcoholics Anonymous.* San Rafael, CA: Paradise Research Publications, 1996.

———. *The Akron Genesis of Alcoholics Anonymous.* 3rd ed. Kihei, HI: Paradise Research Publications, Inc., 1998.

———. *The Books Early AAs Read for Spiritual Growth.* 7th ed., Kihei, HI, CA: Paradise Research Publications, Inc., 1998.

———. *The Good Book and The Big Book: A.A.'s Roots in the Bible.* 2d ed., Kihei, HI: Paradise Research Publications, Inc., 1997.

———, and Bill Pittman. *Courage to Change: The Christian Roots of the 12-Step Movement.* Grand Rapids, MI: Fleming H. Revell, 1994.

———. *Turning Point: A History of Early A.A.'s Spiritual Roots and Successes.* Kihei, HI: Paradise Research Publications, Inc., 1997.

———. *Good Morning! Quiet Time, Morning Watch, Meditation, and Early A.A..* 2d ed. Kihei, HI: Paradise Research Publications, Inc., 1998.

———. *Utilizing Early A.A.'s Spiritual Roots for Recovery Today.* Kihei, HI: Paradise Research Publications, 1998.

B., Jim. *Evolution of Alcoholics Anonymous.* New York: A.A. Archives.

Bishop, Charles, Jr. *The Washingtonians & Alcoholics Anonymous.* WV: The Bishop of Books, 1992.

C., Stewart. *A Reference Guide to the Big Book of Alcoholics Anonymous.* Seattle: Recovery Press, 1986.

Clapp, Charles, Jr. *Drinking's Not the Problem.* New York: Thomas Y. Crowell, 1949.

Conrad, Barnaby. *Time Is All We Have.* New York: Dell Publishing, 1986.

Darrah, Mary C. *Sister Ignatia: Angel of Alcoholics Anonymous.* Chicago: Loyola University Press, 1992.

E., Bob. *Handwritten note to Lois Wilson on pamphlet entitled "Four Absolutes."* (copy made available to the author at Founders Day Archives Room in Akron, Ohio, in June, 1991).

———. Letter from Bob E. to Nell Wing. Stepping Stones Archives.

*First Steps: Al-Anon . . . 35 Years of Beginnings.* New York: Al-Anon Family Group Headquarters, 1986.

Fitzgerald, Robert. *The Soul of Sponsorship: The Friendship of Father Ed Dowling, S.J., and Bill Wilson in Letters.* Center City, Minn.: Hazelden, 1995.

Ford, Betty, with Chris Chase. *The Times of My Life.* New York: Harper and Row, 1978.

Ford, John C. *Depth Psychology, Morality and Alcoholism.* Massachusetts: Weston College, 1951.

Gray, Jerry. *The Third Strike.* Minnesota: Hazelden, 1949.

Hunter, Willard, with assistance from M. D. B. *A.A.'s Roots in the Oxford Group.* New York: A.A. Archives, 1988.

Knippel, Charles T. *Samuel M. Shoemaker's Theological Influence on William G. Wilson's Twelve Step Spiritual Program of Recovery.* Ph. D. dissertation. St. Louis University, 1987.

Kurtz, Ernest. *Not-God: A History of Alcoholics Anonymous.* Exp. ed. Minnesota: Hazelden, 1991.

———. *Shame and Guilt: Characteristics of the Dependency Cycle.* Minnesota: Hazelden, 1981.

Morreim, Dennis C. *Changed Lives: The Story of Alcoholics Anonymous.* Minneapolis: Augsburg Fortress, 1991.

Morse, Robert M, M.D., and Daniel K. Flavin, M.D. "The Definition of Alcoholism." *The Journal of the American Medical Association.* August 26, 1992, pp. 1012-14.

P., Wally. *But, for the Grace of God . . .: How Intergroups & Central Offices Carried the Message of Alcoholics Anonymous in the 1940s.* West Virginia: The Bishop of Books, 1995.

Pittman, Bill. *AA The Way It Began.* Seattle: Glen Abbey Books, 1988.

Poe, Stephen E. and Frances E. *A Concordance to Alcoholics Anonymous.* Nevada: Purple Salamander Press, 1990.

Robertson, Nan. *Getting Better Inside Alcoholics Anonymous.* New York: William Morrow & Co., 1988.

S., Clarence. *Going through the Steps.* 2d ed. Altamonte Springs, FL: Stephen Foreman, 1985.

———. *My Higher Power—The Lightbulb.* 2d ed. Altamonte Springs, FL: Stephen Foreman, 1985.

Seiberling, John F. *Origins of Alcoholics Anonymous.* (A transcript of remarks by Henrietta B. Seiberling: transcript prepared by Congressman John F. Seiberling of a telephone conversation with his mother, Henrietta in the spring of 1971): Employee Assistance Quarterly. 1985; (1); pp. 8-12.

Sikorsky, Igor I., Jr. *AA's Godparents.* Minnesota: CompCare Publishers, 1990.

Smith, Bob and Sue Smith Windows. *Children of the Healer.* Illinois: Parkside Publishing Corporation, 1992.

Thomsen, Robert. *Bill W.* New York: Harper & Row, 1975.

Walker, Richmond. *For Drunks Only.* Minnesota: Hazelden, n.d.

———. *The 7 Points of Alcoholics Anonymous.* Seattle: Glen Abbey Books, 1989.

Webb, Terry. *Tree of Renewed Life: Spiritual Renewal of the Church through the Twelve-Step Program.* New York: Crossroad, 1992.

Wilson, Bill. *How The Big Book Was Put Together.* New York: A.A. General Services Archives, Transcript of Bill Wilson Speech delivered in Fort Worth, Texas, 1954.

———. *Bill Wilson's Original Story.* Bedford Hills, New York: Stepping Stones Archives, n.d., a manuscript whose individual lines are numbered 1 to 1180.

———. "Main Events: Alcoholics Anonymous Fact Sheet by Bill." November 1, 1954. Stepping Stones Archives. Bedford Hills, New York.

———. "The Fellowship of Alcoholics Anonymous." *Quarterly Journal of Studies on Alcohol.* Yale University, 1945, pp. 461-73.

———. *W. G. Wilson Recollections.* Bedford Hills, New York: Stepping Stones Archives, September 1, 1954 transcript of Bill's dictations to Ed B.

Wilson, Jan R., and Judith A. Wilson. *Addictionary: A Primer of Recovery Terms and Concepts from Abstinence to Withdrawal.* New York: Simon and Schuster, 1992.

Wilson, Lois. *Lois Remembers.* New York: Al-Anon Family Group Headquarters, 1987.

Windows, Sue Smith. (daughter of A.A.'s Co-Founder, Dr. Bob). Typewritten Memorandum entitled, *Henrietta and early Oxford Group Friends, by Sue Smith Windows.* Delivered to the author of this book by Sue Smith Windows at Akron, June, 1991.

Wing, Nell. *Grateful to Have Been There: My 42 Years with Bill and Lois, and the Evolution of Alcoholics Anonymous.* Illinois: Parkside Publishing Corporation, 1992.

*Publications Approved by Alcoholics Anonymous*

*Alcoholics Anonymous.* 3rd ed. New York: Alcoholics Anonymous World Services, Inc., 1976.

*Alcoholics Anonymous.* 1st ed. New Jersey: Works Publishing, 1939.

*Alcoholics Anonymous Comes of Age.* New York: Alcoholics Anonymous World Services, Inc., 1957.

*A Newcomer Asks* . . . York, England: A.A. Sterling Area Services, n.d.

*As Bill Sees It: The A.A. Way of Life . . . selected writings of A.A.'s Co-Founder.* New York: Alcoholics Anonymous World Services, Inc., 1967.

*Best of the Grapevine.* New York: The A.A. Grapevine, Inc., 1985.

*Best of the Grapevine, Volume II.* New York: The A.A. Grapevine, Inc., 1986.

*Came to Believe.* New York: Alcoholics Anonymous World Services, Inc., 1973.

*Daily Reflections.* New York: Alcoholics Anonymous World Services, Inc., 1991.

*DR. BOB and the Good Oldtimers.* New York: Alcoholics Anonymous World Services, Inc., 1980.

*44 Questions.* New York: Works Publishing, Inc., 1952.

*Members of the Clergy Ask about Alcoholics Anonymous.* New York: Alcoholics Anonymous World Services, 1961, 1979-revised 1992, according to 1989 Conference Advisory Action.

*Pass It On.* New York: Alcoholics Anonymous World Services, Inc., 1984.

*Questions & Answers on Sponsorship.* New York: Alcoholics Anonymous World Services, Inc., 1976.

*The A.A. Grapevine: "RHS"*—issue dedicated to the memory of the Co-Founder of Alcoholics Anonymous, DR. BOB. New York: A.A. Grapevine, Inc., 1951.

*The A.A. Service Manual.* New York: Alcoholics Anonymous World Services, Inc., 1990-1991.

*The Co-Founders of Alcoholics Anonymous.* New York: Alcoholics Anonymous World Services, Inc., 1972.

*The Language of the Heart.* Bill W.'s Grapevine Writings. New York: The A.A. Grapevine, Inc., 1988.

*This is A.A. . . . An Introduction to the A.A. Recovery Program.* New York: Alcoholics Anonymous World Services, Inc., 1984.

*Twelve Steps and Twelve Traditions.* New York: Alcoholics Anonymous World Services, Inc., 1953.


***Pamphlets Circulated in Early A.A.***


*A.A. God's Instrument.* Chicago: Chicago Area Alcoholics Anonymous Service Office, 1954.

*A. A. Sponsorship: Its Opportunities and Its Responsibilities.* Cleveland: Cleveland Ohio District Office, 1944.

*A Guide to the Twelve Steps of Alcoholics Anonymous.* Akron: AA of Akron, n.d.

*A Guide to Serenity.* Cleveland: The Cleveland District Office of Alcoholics Anonymous, n.d.

*Alcoholics Anonymous: An Interpretation of our Twelve Steps.* Washington, D.C.: Paragon Creative Printers, 1944.

*A Manual for Alcoholics Anonymous.* Akron: AA of Akron, n.d.

*Central Bulletin*, Volumes I - III. Cleveland Central Committee, October, 1942 - December, 1945.

Delahanty, Edward J., M.D. *The Therapeutic Value of the Twelve Steps of A.A.* Salt Lake City, UT: Alcoholism Foundations, n.d.

G., Clyde. *My Quiet Time.* Cleveland: Alcoholics Anonymous, n.d.

*Handles and Hodge Podge*, comp. a member of Alcoholics Anonymous. Cleveland: The Cleveland District Office of Alcoholics Anonymous, n.d.

*Handles for Sobriety*, comp. A Member of Alcoholics Anonymous. Cleveland: The Cleveland District Office of Alcoholics Anonymous, n.d.

*"It's All in the Mind"* Chicago: Chicago Area Alcoholics Anonymous Service Office, n.d.

*Second Reader for Alcoholics Anonymous*. Akron: AA of Akron, n.d.

Smith, Roy. *Emergency Rations*. Cleveland: The Cleveland District Office of Alcoholics Anonymous, n.d.

*Spiritual Milestones in Alcoholics Anonymous*. Akron: A.A. of Akron, n.d.

*The New Way of Life: A.A.* Cleveland: The Cleveland District Office of Alcoholics Anonymous, n.d.

T., John. *A.A.: God's Instrument.* Chicago: Chicago Area Alcoholics Anonymous Service Office, n.d.

*The Devil and A.A.* Chicago: Chicago Area Alcoholics Anonymous Service Office, 1948.

*The Four Absolutes.* Cleveland: Cleveland Central Committee of A.A., n.d.

*The New Way of Life: A.A.* Cleveland: The Cleveland District Office of Alcoholics Anonymous, n.d.

*Twelve Steps of AA and The Bible.* From the collection of Clancy U., n.d.

*What Others Think of A.A.* Akron: Friday Forum Luncheon Club, circa 1941.

Wood, Charles L. *Prayers for Alcoholics.* Cincinnati: Foreword Movement Publications, n.d. From a Midwest Intergroup Office.

### Alcoholics Anonymous: Pro, Con, and Evaluated

*A Program for You: A Guide to the Big Book's Design for Living.* Hazelden Foundation, 1991.

B., Mel. *New Wine: The Spiritual Roots of the Twelve Step Miracle.* Hazelden Foundation, 1991.

Bartosch, Bob and Pauline. *A Bridge to Recovery.* La Habra, CA: Overcomers Outreach, Inc., 1994.

Bishop, Charlie, Jr. and Pittman, Bill. *To Be Continued...The Alcoholics Anonymous World Biography 1935-1994.* Wheeling, WV: The Bishop of Books, 1994.

Bobgan, Martin and Deidre. *12 Steps to Destruction: Codependency Recovery Heresies.* Santa Barbara, CA: EastGate Publishers, 1991.

Bufe, Charles. *Alcoholics Anonymous: Cult or Cure?* San Francisco: Sharp Press, 1991.

Burns, Dr. Cathy. *Alcoholics Anonymous Unmasked: Deception and Deliverance.* Mt. Carmel, PA: Sharing, 1991.

Burns, Robert E., C.S.P. *The Catholic Church and Alcoholics Anonymous.* Columbia, 31: 15-16, May, 1952.

C., Chuck. *A New Pair of Glasses.* Irvine, CA: New-Look Publishing Company, 1984.

Chambers, Cal. *Two Tracks-One Goal: How Alcoholics Anonymous Relates to Christianity.* Langley, B.C., Canada: Credo Publishing Corporation, 1992.

Clinebell, Howard. *Understanding and Counseling Persons with Alcohol, Drug, and Behavioral Addictions.* Rev. and enl. ed. Nashville: Abingdon Press, 1998.

Costantino, Frank. *Holes in Time: The Autobiography of a Gangster.* 2d ed. Dallas, TX: Acclaimed Books, 1986.

Cunningham, Loren. *Is That Really You, God?: Hearing the Voice of God.* Seattle, WA: YWAM Publishing, 1984.

Davis, Martin M. *The Gospel and the Twelve Steps: Developing a Closer Relationship with Jesus.* San Diego, CA: Recovery Publications, Inc., 1993.

Dowling, The Reverend Edward, S.J. *Catholic Asceticism and the Twelve Steps*. St. Louis, MO, The Queen's Work, Brooklyn, 1953.

Doyle, Paul Barton. *In Step with God: A Scriptural Guide for Practicing 12 Step Programs*. Brentwood, TN: New Directions, 1989.

Dunn, Jerry G. *God is for the Alcoholic*. Chicago: Moody Press, 1965.

Fingarette, Herbert. *Heavy Drinking: The Myth of Alcoholism as a Disease*. Berkeley, CA: University of California Press, 1988.

Fitzgerald, Robert. *The Soul of Sponsorship: The Friendship of Fr. Ed Dowling, S.J. and Bill Wilson in Letters*. Hazelden, 1995.

Hemfelt, Robert and Fowler, Richard. *Serenity: A Companion for Twelve Step Recovery*. Nashville, TN: Thomas Nelson Publishers, 1990.

Jellinek, E. M. *The Disease Concept of Alcoholism*. New Haven, CN: College and University Press, 1960.

Kessel, Joseph. *The Road Back: A Report on Alcoholics Anonymous*. New York: Alfred A. Knopf, 1962.

Kurtz, Ernest and Ketcham, Katherine. *The Spirituality of Imperfection: Modern Wisdom from Classic Stories*. New York: Bantam Books, 1992.

Landry, Mim J. *Overview of Addiction Treatment Effectiveness*. Rev.ed., 1997. U.S. Department of Health and Human Services.

Larson, Joan Mathews. *Seven Weeks to Sobriety: The Proven Program to Fight Alcoholism Through Nutrition*. New York: Fawcett Columbine, 1992

McQ., Joe. *The Steps We Took*. Little Rock, AR: August House Publishers, Inc., 1990.

Miller, J. Keith. *A Hunger for Healing: The Twelve Steps as a Classic Model for Christian Spiritual Growth*. San Francisco: HarperSanFrancisco, 1991.

O., Dr. Paul. *There's more to Quitting Drinking than Quitting Drinking*. Laguna Niguel, CA: Sabrina Publishing, 1995.

P., Wally. *Back to Basics: The Alcoholics Anonymous Beginners' Classes. Take all 12 Steps in Four One-Hour Sessions*. Tucson, AZ: Faith With Works Publishing Company, 1997.

Parham, A. Philip. *Letting God: Christian Meditations for Recovering Persons*. San Francisco: Harper & Row, 1987.

Peale, Norman Vincent. *The Positive Power of Jesus Christ: Life-Changing Adventures in Faith*. Pauling, NY: Foundation for Christian Living, 1980.

———. *The Power of Positive Thinking*. Pauling, NY: Peale Center for Christian Living, 1978.

Playfair, William L. *The Useful Lie*. Wheaton, IL: Crossway Books, 1991.

Ragge, Ken. *More Revealed: A Critical Analysis of Alcoholics Anonymous and the Twelve Steps*. Henderson, NV: Alert! Publishing, 1991.

*Life Recovery Bible, The: The Living Bible*. Wheaton, IL: Tyndale House Publishers, Inc., 1992.

Seiden, Jerry. *Divine or Distorted?: God As We Understand God*. San Diego, CA: Recovery Publications, Inc., 1993.

*Self-Help Sourcebook, The: Your Guide to Community and Online Support Groups*. 6th.ed. compiled and edited by Barbara J. White and Edward J. Madara. Denville, NJ: American Self-Help Clearinghouse, 1994.

Shoemaker, Samuel M., Jr. *Revive Thy Church Beginning with Me*. New York: Harper & Brothers, 1948.

———. *The Church Alive*. New York: E. P. Dutton, 1951.

Stafford, Tim. *The Hidden Gospel of the 12 Steps*. *Christianity Today*, July 22, 1991.

Trimpey, Jack. *Rational Recovery: The New Cure for Substance Addiction*. New York: Pocket Books, 1996.

———. *Revolutionary Alternative for Overcoming Alcohol and Drug Dependence, A: The Small Book*. Rev. ed. NY: Delacorte Press, 1992.

U.S. Department of Health and Human Services. Substance Abuse and Mental Health Services Administration. *National Household Survey on Drug Abuse: Main Findings 1996*. Rockville, MD: SAMHSA, Office of Applied Studies, 1998.

Vaillant, George E. *The Natural History of Alcoholism Revisited*. Cambridge, MA: Harvard University Press, 1995.

*Way Home, The: A Spiritual Approach to Recovery*. Orlando, FL: Bridge Builders, Inc., 1996.

White, William L. *Slaying The Dragon: The History of Addiction Treatment and Recovery in America*. Bloomington, IL: Chestnut Health Systems/Lighthouse Institute, 1998

Wing, Nell. *Grateful to have Been There: My 42 Years with Bill and Lois and the Evolution of Alcoholics Anonymous*. Park Ridge, IL: Parkside Publishing Corporation, 1992.

## The Bible—Versions of and Books About

*Authorized King James Version*. New York: Thomas Nelson, 1984.

Benson, Clarence H. *A Popular History of Christian Education*. Chicago: Moody Press.

Bullinger, Ethelbert W. *A Critical Lexicon and Concordance to the English and Greek New Testament*. Michigan: Zondervan, 1981.

Burns, Kenneth Charles. "The Rhetoric of Christology." Master's thesis, San Francisco State University, 1991.

*Every Catholic's Guide to the Sacred Scriptures*. Nashville: Thomas Nelson, 1990.

Gray, James M. Synthetic Bible Studies: Containing an Outline Study of Every Book of the Bible, With Suggestions for Sermons, Addresses and Bible Expositions. New York: Fleming H. Revell Company.

Harnack, Adolph. *The Expansion of Christianity in the First Three Centuries*. New York: G. P. Putnam's Sons, Volume I, 1904; Volume II, 1905.

Jukes, Andrew. *The Names of GOD in Holy Scripture*. Michigan: Kregel Publications, 1967.

Kohlenberger, John R., III, gen. ed. *The Contemporary Parallel New Testament*. New York: Oxford University Press, 1997.

Mau, Charles P. *James M. Gray As a Christian Educator*. Master's thesis, Fuller Theological Seminary, 1963.

Megivern, James J. *Official Catholic Teachings: Bible Interpretation*. North Carolina: McGrath Publishing Company, 1978.

Moffatt, James. *A New Translation of the Bible*. New York: Harper & Brothers, 1954.

*New Bible Dictionary*. 2d ed. Wheaton, Illinois: Tyndale House Publishers, 1987.

On, J. Edwin. *Full Surrender*. London: Marshall, Morgan & Scott, 1951.

Phillips, J. B. *The New Testament in Modern English*. New York: The Macmillan Company, 1958.

Puskas, Charles B. *An Introduction to the New Testament*. Mass.: Hendrickson Publishers, 1989.

*Recovery Devotional Bible*. Grand Rapids, MI: Zondervan Publishing House, 1993.

*Revised Standard Version*. New York: Thomas Nelson, 1952.

*Serenity: A Companion for Twelve Step Recovery*. Nashville: Thomas Nelson, 1990.

Schaff, Philip. *History of the Christian Church*. Grand Rapids, MI: Wm. B. Eerdmans, Volume II, 1956.

Strong, James. *The Exhaustive Concordance of the Bible*. Iowa: Riverside Book and Bible House, n.d.

*The Abingdon Bible Commentary*. New York: Abingdon Press, 1929.

*The Companion Bible*. Michigan: Zondervan Bible Publishers, 1964.

*The Life Recovery Bible*. Wheaton, IL: Tyndale House Publishers, 1992.

*The Revised English Bible*. Oxford: Oxford University Press, 1989.

Vine, W. E. *Vine's Expository Dictionary of Old and New Testament Words*. New York: Fleming H. Revell, 1981.

*Young's Analytical Concordance to the Bible*. New York: Thomas Nelson, 1982.

Zodhiates, Spiros. *The Hebrew-Greek Key Study Bible*. 6th ed. AMG Publishers, 1991.

## Bible Devotionals

Chambers, Oswald. *My Utmost for His Highest*. London: Simpkin Marshall, Ltd., 1927.

Clark, Glenn, *I Will Lift Up Mine Eyes*. New York: Harper & Brothers, 1937.

Dunnington, Lewis L. *Handles of Power*. New York: Abingdon-Cokesbury Press, 1942.

Fosdick, Harry Emerson. *The Meaning of Prayer*. New York: Association Press, 1915.

Holm, Nora Smith. *The Runner's Bible*. New York: Houghton Mifflin Company, 1915.

Jones, E. Stanley. *Abundant Living*. New York: Abingdon-Cokesbury Press, 1942.

———. *Victorious Living*. New York: Abingdon Press, 1936.

Parham, A. Philip. *Letting God: Christian Meditations for Recovering Persons*. New York: Harper & Row, 1987.

Prescott, D. M. *A New Day: Daily Readings for Our Time*. New ed. London: Grosvenor Books, 1979.

*The Upper Room: Daily Devotions for Family and Individual Use*. Quarterly. 1st issue: April, May, June, 1935. Edited by Grover Carlton Emmons. Nashville: General Committee on Evangelism through the Department of Home Missions, Evangelism, Hospitals, Board of Missions, Methodist Episcopal Church, South.

The Two Listeners. *God Calling*. Edited by A. J. Russell. Australia: DAYSTAR, 1953.

Tileston, Mary W. *Daily Strength for Daily Needs*. Boston: Roberts Brothers, 1893.

## Publications by or about the Oxford Group & Oxford Group People

*A Day in Pennsylvania Honoring Frank Nathan Daniel Buchman in Pennsburg and Allentown.* Oregon: Grosvenor Books, 1992.

Allen, Geoffrey Francis. *He That Cometh.* New York: The Macmillan Company, 1933.

Almond, Harry J. *Foundations for Faith.* 2d ed. London: Grosvenor Books, 1980.

———. *Iraqi Statesman: A Portrait of Mohammed Fadhel Jamali.* Salem, OR: Grosvenor Books, 1993.

Austin, H. W. "Bunny". *Frank Buchman As I Knew Him.* London: Grosvenor Books, 1975.

———. *Moral Re-Armament: The Battle for Peace.* London: William Heinemann, 1938.

Batterson, John E. *How to Listen to God.* N.p., n.d.

Bayless, W. N. *The Oxford Group: A Way of Life,* n.d.

Becker, Mrs. George. "Quiet Time in the Home." N.p., n.d.

Begbie, Harold. *Life Changers.* New York: G. P. Putnam's Sons, 1927.

———. *Souls in Action.* New York: Hodder & Stoughton, 1911.

———. *Twice-Born Men.* New York: Fleming H. Revell, 1909.

Belden, David C. *The Origins and Development of the Oxford Group (Moral Re-Armament).* D. Phil. Dissertation, Oxford University, 1976.

Belden, Kenneth D. *Beyond The Satellites: Is God is Speaking-Are We Listening?* London: Grosvenor Books, 1987.

———. *Meeting Moral Re-Armament.* London: Grosvenor Books, 1979.

———. *Reflections on Moral Re-Armament.* London: Grosvenor Books, 1983.

———. *The Hour of the Helicopter.* Somerset, England: Linden Hall, 1992.

Bennett, John C. *Social Salvation.* New York: Charles Scribner's Sons, 1935.

Benson, Clarence Irving. *The Eight Points of the Oxford Group.* London: Humphrey Milford, Oxford University Press, 1936.

Blair, David. *For Tomorrow-Yes!* Compiled and edited from David Blair's Notebook by Jane Mullen Blair & Friends. New York: Exposition Press, 1981.

Blair, Emily Newell. "The Oxford Group Challenges America." *Good Housekeeping,* October, 1936.

Blake, Howard C. *Way to Go: Adventures in Search of God's Will.* Burbank, CA: Pooh Stix Press, 1992.

Braden, Charles Samuel. *These Also Believe.* New York: The Macmillan Company, 1951.

Brown, Philip Marshall. *The Venture of Belief.* New York: Fleming H. Revell, 1935.

Buchman, Frank N. D. *Remaking the World.* London: Blandford Press, 1961.

———, and Sherwood Eddy. *Ten Suggestions for Personal Work* (not located).

———. *The Revolutionary Path: Moral Re-Armament in the thinking of Frank Buchman.* London: Grosvenor, 1975.

———. *Where Personal Work Begins.* Extracts and notes from talks given at the Lily Valley Conference near Kuling, China 1-13 August, 1918. London: Grosvenor Books, 1984.

*Frank Buchman-80.* Compiled by His Friends. London: Blandford Press, 1958.

Bundy, David D. *Keswick: A Bibliographic Introduction to the Higher Life Movements.* Wilmore, Kentucky: B. L. Fisher Library of Asbury Theological Seminary, 1975.

————. "Keswick and the Experience of Evangelical Piety." Chap. 7 in *Modern Christian Revivals*. Urbana, IL: University of Illinois Press, 1992.

Campbell, Paul. *The Art of Remaking Men*. Bombay: Himmat Publications, 1970.

————. *The Strategy of St. Paul*. London: Grosvenor Books, 1956.

————, and Peter Howard. *Remaking Men*. New York: Arrowhead Books, 1954.

Cantrill, Hadley. *The Psychology of Social Movements*. New York: John Wiley & Sons, Inc., 1941.

Carey, Walter, Bishop of Bloemfontein. *The Group System and the Catholic Church*. Archives of the Episcopal Church, Austin, Texas, n.d.

Chesteron, G. K. *The Well and The Shallows*, circa 1935, pp. 435-39.

Clapp, Charles, Jr. *The Big Bender*. New York: Harper & Row, 1938.

————. *Drinking's Not the Problem*. New York: Thomas Y. Crowell, 1949.

Clark, Walter Houston. *The Oxford Group: Its History and Significance*. New York: Bookman Associates, 1951.

Cook, Sydney and Garth Lean. *The Black and White Book: A Handbook of Revolution*. London: Blandford Press, 1972.

Crossman, R. H. S. *Oxford and the Groups*. Oxford: Basil Blackwell, 1934.

Crothers, Susan. *Susan and God*. New York: Harper & Brothers, 1939.

Day, Sherwood Sunderland. *The Principles of the Group*. Oxford: University Press, n.d.

Dayton, Donald W., ed. *The Higher Christian Life: Sources for the Study of the Holiness, Pentecostal and Keswick Movements*. New York: Garland Publishing, 1984.

Dinger, Clair M. *Moral Re-Armament: A Study of Its Technical and Religious Nature in the Light of Catholic Teaching*. Washington, D.C.: The Catholic University of America Press, 1961.

"Discord in Oxford Group: Buchmanites Ousted by Disciple from N.Y. Parish House." *Newsweek*. November 24, 1941.

Dorsey, Theodore H. *From a Far Country: The Conversion Story of a Campaigner for Christ*. Huntington, Indiana: Our Sunday Visitor Press, n.d.

Drakeford, John W. *People to People Therapy*. New York: Harper & Row, 1978.

Driberg, Tom. *The Mystery of Moral Re-Armament: A Study of Frank Buchman and His Movement*. New York: Alfred A. Knopf, 1965.

du Maurier, Daphne. *Come Wind, Come Weather*. London: William Heinemann, 1941.

Entwistle, Basil, and John McCook Roots. *Moral Re-Armament: What Is It?* Pace Publications, 1967.

Eister, Allan W. *Drawing Room Conversion*. Durham: Duke University Press, 1950.

Ferguson, Charles W. *The Confusion of Tongues*. Garden City: Doubleday, Doran Company, Inc., 1940.

Foot, Stephen. *Life Began Yesterday*. New York: Harper & Brothers, 1935.

Ford, John C., S.J. *Moral Re-Armament and Alcoholics Anonymous*. NCCA "Blue Book," Vol 10, 1968.

Forde, Eleanor Napier. *Guidance: What It Is and How to Get It*. Paper presented by Eleanor Napier Forde at Minnewaska, NY, September, 1927.

————. *The Guidance of God*. London: The Oxford Group, 1927.

Gordon, Anne Wolrige. *Peter Howard, Life and Letters*. London: Hodder & Stoughton, 1969.

Gray, Betty. *Watersheds: Journey to a faith*. London: Grosvenor, 1986.

Grensted, L. W. *The Person of Christ*. New York: Harper & Brothers, 1933.

Grogan, William. *John Riffe of the Steelworkers*. New York: Coward—McCann, 1959.

Hadden, Richard M. "Christ's Program for World-Reconstruction: Studies in the Sermon on the Mount." *The Calvary Evangel*, 1934-35, pp. 11-14, 44-49, 73-77, 104-07, 133-36.

Hamilton, A. S. Loudon. *MRA: How It All Began*. London: Moral Re-Armament, 1968.

———. *Some Basic Principles of Christian Work*. The Oxford Group, n.d.

———. "Description of the First Century Christian Fellowship." Vol. 2, *The Messenger*, June, 1923.

Hamlin, Bryan T. *Moral Re-Armament and Forgiveness in International Affairs*. London: Grosvenor, 1992.

Harris, Irving. *An Outline of the Life of Christ*. New York: The Oxford Group, 1935.

———. *Out in Front: Forerunners of Christ. A Study of the Lives of Eight Great Men*. New York: The Calvary Evangel, 1942.

———. *The Breeze of the Spirit*. New York: The Seabury Press, 1978.

Harrison, Marjorie. *Saints Run Mad*. London: John Lane, Ltd., 1934.

Henderson, Michael. *A Different Accent*. Richmond, VA: Grosvenor Books USA, 1985.

———. *All Her Paths Are Peace: Women Pioneers in Peacemaking*. CT: Kumerian Press, 1994.

———. *Hope for a Change: Commentaries by an Optimistic Realist*. Salem, OR: Grosvenor Books, 1991.

———. *On History's Coattails: Commentaries by an English Journalist in America*. Richmond, VA: Grosvenor USA, 1988.

Henson, Herbert Hensley. *The Oxford Group Movement*. London: Oxford University Press, 1933.

Hicks, Roger. *How Augustine Found Faith: Told in his own words from F. J. Sheed's translation of The Confessions of St. Augustine*. N.p., 1956.

———. *How to Read the Bible*. London: Moral Re-Armament, 1940.

———. *Letters to Parsi*. London: Blandford Press, 1960.

———. *The Endless Adventure*. London: Blandford Press, 1964.

———. *The Lord's Prayer and Modern Man*. London: Blandford Press, 1967.

Hofmeyr, Bremer. *How to Change*. New York: Moral Re-Armament, n.d.

———. *How to Listen*. London: The Oxford Group, 1941.

Holme, Reginald. *A Journalist for God: The memoirs of Reginald Holme*. London: A Bridge Builders Publication, 1995.

Holmes-Walker, Wilfrid. *The New Enlistment*. London: The Oxford Group, circa 1937.

Howard, Peter. *Frank Buchman's Secret*. Garden City: New York: Doubleday & Company, Inc., 1961.

———. *Fighters Ever*. London: William Heinemann, 1941

———. *Innocent Men*. London: William Heinemann, 1941.

———. *Ideas Have Legs*. London: Muller, 1945.

———. *That Man Frank Buchman*. London: Blandford Press, 1946.

———. *The World Rebuilt*. New York. Duell, Sloan & Pearce, 1951.

Hunter, T. Willard, with assistance from M.D.B. *A.A.'s Roots in the Oxford Group*. New York: A.A. Archives, 1988.

———. *Press Release*. Buchman Events/Pennsylvania, October 19, 1991.

———. *"It Started Right There" Behind the Twelve Steps and the Self-help Movement.* Oregon: Grosvenor Books, 1994.

———. *The Spirit of Charles Lindbergh: Another Dimension.* Lanham, MD: Madison Books, 1993.

———. *Uncommon Friends' Uncommon Friend.* A tribute to James Draper Newton, on the occasion of his eighty-fifth birthday. (Pamphlet, March 30, 1990).

———. *World Changing Through Life Changing.* Thesis, Newton Center, Mass: Andover-Newton Theological School, 1977.

Hutchinson, Michael. *A Christian Approach to Other Faiths.* London: Grosvenor Books, 1991.

———. *The Confessions.* (privately published study of St. Augustine's *Confessions*).

Jaeger, Clara. *Philadelphia Rebel: The Education of a Bourgeoise.* Virginia: Grosvenor, 1988.

Jones, Olive M. *Inspired Children.* New York: Harper & Brothers, 1933.

———. *Inspired Youth.* New York: Harper & Brothers, 1938.

Kitchen, V. C. *I Was a Pagan.* New York: Harper & Brothers, 1934.

Kestne, Eugene. *The Lord of History.* Boston: Daughters of St. Paul, 1980.

Koenig, His Eminence Franz Cardinal. *True Dialogue.* Oregon: Grosvenor USA, 1986.

Laun, Ferdinand. *Unter Gottes Fuhring.* The Oxford Group, n.d.

Lean, Garth. *Cast Out Your Nets.* London: Grosvenor, 1990.

———. *Frank Buchman: A Life.* London: Constable, 1985.

———. *Good God, It Works.* London: Blandford Press, 1974.

———. *Joyful Remembrance.* London: Executors of Garth D. Lean, 1994.

———. *On the Tail of a Comet: The Life of Frank Buchman.* Colorado Springs: Helmers & Howard, 1988.

———, and Morris Martin. *New Leadership.* London: William Heinemann, 1936.

Leon, Philip. A Philosopher's Quiet Time. N.p., n.d.

———. *The Philosophy of Courage or the Oxford Group Way.* New York: Oxford University Press, 1939.

"Less Buchmanism." *Time*, November 24, 1941.

*Letter 7, The: The South African Adventure. A Miracle Working God Abroad.* Oxford: The Groups, A First Century Christian Fellowship, 1930.

Macintosh, Douglas C. *Personal Religion.* New York: Charles Scribner's Sons, 1942.

Mackay, Malcom George. *More than Coincidence.* Edinburgh: The Saint Andrew Press, 1979.

Macmillan, Ebenezer. *Seeking and Finding.* New York: Harper & Brothers, 1933.

Margetson, The Very Reverend Provost. *The South African Adventure.* The Oxford Group, n.d.

Martin, Morris H. *The Thunder and the Sunshine.* Washington D.C.: MRA, n.d.

———. *Born to Live in the Future.* n.l.: Up With People, 1991.

McAll, Dr. Frances. *So what's the alternative?* London: Moral Re-Armament, 1974.

Molony, John N. *Moral Re-Armament.* Melbourne: The Australian Catholic Truth Society Record, June 10, 1956.

Mottu, Philippe. *The Story of Caux.* London: Grosvenor, 1970.

Mowat, R. C. *Modern Prophetic Voices: From Kierkegaard to Buchman.* Oxford: New Cherwel Press, 1994.

———. *The Message of Frank Buchman*. London: Blandford Press, n.d.

———. *Report on Moral Re-Armament*. London: Blandford Press, 1955.

———. *Creating the European Community*. London, 1973.

———. *Decline and Renewal: Europe Ancient and Modern*. Oxford: New Cherwel Press, 1991.

Moyes, John S. *American Journey*. Sydney: Clarendon Publishing Co., n. d.

Murray, Robert H. *Group Movements Throughout the Ages*. New York: Harper & Brothers. 1935.

Newton, Eleanor Forde. *I Always Wanted Adventure*. London: Grosvenor, 1992.

———. *Echoes From The Heart*. Fort Myers Beach, Florida, 1986.

Newton, James Draper. *Uncommon Friends: Life with Thomas Edison, Henry Ford, Harvey Firestone, Alexis Carrel, & Charles Lindbergh*. New York: Harcourt Brace, 1987.

Nichols, Beverley. *The Fool Hath Said*. Garden City: Doubleday, Doran & Company, 1936.

Orglmeister, Peter. *An Ideology for Today*. Pamphlet, 1965.

Perry, Edward T. *God Can Be Real*. Moral Re-Armament, Inc., 1969.

Petrocokino, Paul. *The New Man for the New World*. Cheshire: Paul Petrocokino, n.d.

———. *The Right Direction*. Great Britain: The City Press of Chester, Ltd., n.d.

———. *An Experiment: Try This For a Fortnight*. Privately published pamphlet, n.d.

Phillimore, Miles. *Just for Today*. Privately published pamphlet, 1940.

Prescott, D. M. *A New Day: Daily Readings for Our Time*. New ed. London: Grosvenor Book, 1979.

Raynor, Frank D., and Leslie D. Weatherhead. *The Finger of God*. London: Group Publications, Ltd., 1934.

Reynolds, Amelia S. *New Lives for Old*. New York. Fleming H. Revell, 1929.

Roots, The Right Reverend Herbert, Bishop of Hankow, China. *The Two Options*. The Oxford Group, 1934.

Roots, John McCook. *An Apostle to Youth*. Oxford, The Oxford Group, 1928.

Rose, Cecil. *When Man Listens*. New York: Oxford University Press, 1937.

Rose, Howard J. *The Quiet Time*. New York: Oxford Group at 61 Gramercy Park, North, 1937.

Russell, Arthur J. *For Sinners Only*. London: Hodder & Stoughton, 1932.

———. *One Thing I Know*. New York: Harper & Brothers, 1933.

Sangster, W. E. *God Does Guide Us*. New York: The Abingdon Press, 1934.

Sherry, Frank H. and Mahlon H. Hellerich. *The Formative Years of Frank N. D. Buchman*. (Reprint of article at Frank Buchman home in Allentown, Pennsylvania).

Spencer, F. A. M. *The Meaning of the Groups*. London: Methuen & Co., Ltd., 1934.

Spoerri, Theophil. *Dynamic out of Silence: Frank Buchman's Relevance Today*. Translated by John Morrison. London: Grosvenor Books, 1976.

Streeter, Burnett Hillman. *The God Who Speaks*. London: Macmillan & Co., Ltd., 1936.

———. *Reality*. London, 1943.

Suenens, Rt. Rev. Msgr. *The Right View of Moral Re-Armament*. London: Burns and Oates, 1952.

The Bishop of Leicester, Chancellor R. J. Campbell and the Editor of the "Church of England Newspaper." *Stories of our Oxford House Party.*, July 17, 1931.

*The Groups in South Africa 1930*. South Africa: The Groups, 1930.

The Layman with a Notebook. *What Is the Oxford Group?* London: Oxford University Press, 1933.

Thornhill, Alan. *One Fight More*. London: Frederick Muller, 1943.

———. *The Significance of the Life of Frank Buchman*. London: Moral Re-Armament, 1952.

———. *Best of Friends: A Life of Enriching Friendships*. United Kingdom, Marshall Pickering, 1986.

Thornton-Duesbury, Julian P. *Sharing*. The Oxford Group. n.d.

———. *The Oxford Group: A Brief Account of its Principles and Growth*. London: The Oxford Group, 1947.

———. *The Open Secret of MRA*. London: Blandford, 1964.

———. *A Visit to Caux: First-hand experience of Moral Re-Armament in action*. London: The Oxford Group, 1960.

"Calvary's Eviction of Buchman." *Time Magazine*, November 24, 1941.

Twitchell, Kenaston. *Do You Have to Be Selfish*. New York: Moral Re-Armament, n.d.

———. *How Do You Make Up Your Mind*. New York: Moral Re-Armament, n.d.

———. *Regeneration in the Ruhr*. Princeton: Princeton University Press, 1981.

———. *Supposing Your Were Absolutely Honest*. New York: Moral Re-Armament, n.d.

———. *The Strength of a Nation: Absolute Purity*. New York: Moral Re-Armament, n.d.

Van Dusen, Henry P. "Apostle to the Twentieth Century: Frank N. D. Buchman." *The Atlantic Monthly*, Vol. 154, pp. 1-16 (July 1934).

———. "The Oxford Group Movement: An Appraisal." *The Atlantic Monthly*. Vol. 154, pp. 230-252 (August 1934).

Viney, Hallen. *How Do I Begin?* The Oxford Group, 61 Gramercy Park, New York., 1937.

Vrooman, Lee. *The Faith That Built America*. New York: Arrowhead Books, Inc., 1955.

Waddy, Charis. *The Skills of Discernment*. London: Grosvenor Books, 1977.

Walter, Howard A. *Soul Surgery: Some Thoughts On Incisive Personal Work*. Oxford: The Oxford Group, 1928.

Watt, Frederick B. *Great Bear: A Journey Remembered*. Yellowknife, Northwest Territories, Canada: The Northern Publishers, 1980.

Weatherhead, Leslie D. *Discipleship*. London: Student Christian Movement Press, 1934.

———. *How Can I Find God?* London: Fleming H. Revell, 1934.

———. *Psychology and Life*. New York: Abingdon Press, 1935.

West, The Right Rev. George. *The World That Works*. London: Blandford, 1945.

Williamson, Geoffrey. *Inside Buchmanism*. New York: Philosophical Library, Inc., 1955.

Winslow, Jack C. *Church in Action* (no data available to author).

———. *Vital Touch with God: How to Carry on Adequate Devotional Life*. The Evangel, 8 East 40th St., New York, n.d.

———. *When I Awake*. London: Hodder & Stoughton, 1938.

———. *Why I Believe in the Oxford Group*. London: Hodder & Stoughton, 1934.

**Books by or about Oxford Group Mentors**

Bushnell, Horace. *The New Life*. London: Strahan & Co., 1868.

Chapman, J. Wilbur. *Life and Work of Dwight L. Moody*. Philadelphia, 1900.

Cheney, Mary B. *Life and Letters of Horace Bushnell*. New York: Harper & Brothers, 1890.

Drummond, Henry. *Essays and Addresses*. New York: James Potts & Company, 1904.

————. *Natural Law in the Spiritual World*. Potts Edition.

————. *The Changed Life*. New York: James Potts & Company, 1891.

————. *The Greatest Thing in the World and Other Addresses*. London: Collins, 1953.

————. *The Ideal Life*. London: Hodder & Stoughton, 1897.

————. *The New Evangelism and Other Papers*. London: Hodder & Stoughton, 1899.

Edwards, Robert L. *Of Singular Genius, of Singular Grace: A Biography of Horace Bushnell*. Cleveland: The Pilgrim Press, 1992.

Findlay, James F., Jr. *Dwight L. Moody American Evangelist*. Chicago, University of Chicago Press, 1969.

Fitt, Emma Moody, *Day by Day with D. L. Moody*. Chicago: Moody Press, n.d.

Goodspeed, Edgar J. *The Wonderful Career of Moody and Sankey in Great Britain and America*. New York: Henry S. Goodspeed & Co., 1876.

Guldseth, Mark O. *Streams*. Alaska: Fritz Creek Studios, 1982.

Hopkins, C. Howard. *John R. Mott, a Biography*. Grand Rapids: William B. Erdmans Publishing Company, 1979.

James, William. *The Varieties of Religious Experience*. New York: First Vintage Books/The Library of America, 1990.

Meyer, F. B. *Five Musts*. Chicago: Moody Press, 1927.

————. *The Secret of Guidance*. New York: Fleming H. Revell, 1896.

Moody, Paul D. *My Father: An Intimate Portrait of Dwight Moody*. Boston: Little Brown, 1938.

Moody, William R. *The Life of D. L. Moody*. New York: Fleming H. Revell, 1900.

Mott, John R. *The Evangelization of the World in This Generation*. London, 1901.

————. *Addresses and Papers* (no further data at this time).

————. *Five Decades and a Forward View*. 4th ed. New York: Harper & Brothers, 1939.

Pollock, J. C. *Moody: A Biographical Portrait of the Pacesetter in Modern Mass Evangelism*. New York: Macmillan, 1963.

Smith, George Adam. *The Life of Henry Drummond*. New York: McClure, Phillips & Co., 1901.

Speer, Robert E. *Studies of the Man Christ Jesus*. New York: Fleming H. Revell, 1896.

————. *The Marks of a Man*. New York: Hodder & Stoughton, 1907.

————. *The Principles of Jesus*. New York: Fleming H. Revell Company, 1902.

Stewart, George, Jr. *Life of Henry B. Wright*. New York: Association Press, 1925.

Wright, Henry B. *The Will of God and a Man's Lifework*. New York: The Young Men's Christian Association Press, 1909.

## Publications by or about Samuel Moor Shoemaker, Jr.

Shoemaker, Samuel Moor, Jr., "A 'Christian Program.'" In *Groups That Work: The Key to Renewal . . . for Churches, Communities, and Individuals.* Compiled by Walden Howard and the Editors of Faith At Work. Michigan: Zondervan, 1967.
———. "Act As If." *Christian Herald.* October, 1954.
———. "A First Century Christian Fellowship: A Defense of So-called Buchmanism by One of Its Leaders." Reprinted from the *Churchman*, circa 1928.
———. "And So from My Heart I Say . . ." *The A.A. Grapevine.* New York: The A.A. Grapevine, Inc., September, 1948.
———. *. . . And Thy Neighbor.* Waco, Texas: Word Books, 1967.
———. *A Young Man's View of the Ministry.* New York: Association Press, 1923.
———. *Beginning Your Ministry.* New York: Harper & Row Publishers, 1963.
———. *By the Power of God.* New York: Harper & Brothers, 1954.
———. *Calvary Church Yesterday and Today.* New York: Fleming H. Revell, 1936.
———. *Children of the Second Birth.* New York: Fleming H. Revell, 1927.
———. *Christ and This Crisis.* New York: Fleming H. Revell, 1943.
———. *Christ's Words from the Cross.* New York: Fleming H. Revell, 1933.
———. *Confident Faith.* New York: Fleming H. Revell, 1932.
———. *Extraordinary Living for Ordinary Men.* Michigan: Zondervan, 1965.
———. *Faith at Work.* A symposium edited by Samuel Moor Shoemaker. Hawthorne Books, 1958.
———. *Freedom and Faith.* New York: Fleming H. Revell, 1949.
———. *God and America.* New York: Book Stall, 61 Gramercy Park North, New York, n.d.
———. *God's Control.* New York: Fleming H. Revell, 1939.
———. *How to Become a Christian.* New York: Harper & Brothers, 1953.
———. "How to Find God." *The Calvary Evangel.* July, 1957, pp. 1-24.
———. *How to Help People.* Cincinnati: Forward Movement Publications, 1976.
———. *How You Can Find Happiness.* New York: E. P. Dutton & Co., 1947.
———. *How You Can Help Other People.* New York: E. P. Dutton & Co., 1946.
———. *If I Be Lifted Up.* New York: Fleming H. Revell, 1931.
———. *In Memoriam: The Service of Remembrance.* Princeton: The Graduate Council, Princeton University, June 10, 1956.
———. *Living Your Life Today.* New York: Fleming H. Revell, 1947.
———. "Lord, Teach Us to Pray." *Creative Help for Daily Living* (Foundation for Christian Living, Pawling, New York) 28, no. 2 (1977), Part ii.
———. *Morning Radio Talk No. 1, by Reverend Samuel M. Shoemaker*, American Broadcasting Co., 1 page transcript of program for October 4, 1945.
———. *My Life-Work and My Will.* Pamphlet, Christian ministry conference, Concord, N.H., circa 1930.
———. *National Awakening.* New York: Harper & Brothers, 1936.
———. *One Boy's Influence.* New York: Association Press, 1925.
———. *Realizing Religion.* New York: Association Press, 1923.
———. *Religion That Works.* New York: Fleming H. Revell, 1928.
———. *Revive Thy Church.* New York: Harper & Brothers, 1948.

————. *Sam Shoemaker at His Best*. New York: Faith At Work, 1964.

————. *So I Stand by the Door and Other Verses*. Pittsburgh: Calvary Rectory, 1958.

————. *Steps of a Modern Disciple*. Atlanta, GA: Lay Renewal Publications, 1972.

————. *The Breadth and Narrowness of the Gospel*. New York: Fleming H. Revell, 1929.

————. *The Calvary Evangel, monthly articles in*. New York. Calvary Episcopal Church.

————. *The Church Alive*. New York: E. P. Dutton & Co., Inc., 1951.

————. *The Church Can Save the World*. New York: Harper & Brothers, 1938.

————. *The Conversion of the Church*. New York: Fleming H. Revell, 1932.

————. "The Crisis of Self-Surrender." *Guideposts*. November, 1955.

————. *The Experiment of Faith*. New York: Harper & Brothers. 1957.

————. *The Gospel According to You*. New York: Fleming H. Revell, 1934.

————. *The James Houston Eccleston Day-Book: Containing a Short Account of His Life and Readings for Every Day in the Year Chosen from His Sermons*. Compiled by Samuel M. Shoemaker, Jr. New York: Longmans, Green & Co., 1915.

————. "The Spiritual Angle." *The A.A. Grapevine*. New York: The A.A. Grapevine, Inc., October, 1955.

————. "The Way to Find God." *The Calvary Evangel* (August, 1935).

————. *They're on the Way*. New York: E. P. Dutton, 1951.

————. "Creative Relationships." In *Together*. New York: Abingdon Cokesbury Press, 1946.

————. "The Twelve Steps of A.A.: What They Can Mean to the Rest of Us." *The Calvary Evangel*. New York: The Evangel, 1953.

————. "Those Twelve Steps As I Understand Them." *Best of the Grapevine: Volume II*. New York: The A.A. Grapevine, Inc., 1986.

————. "12 Steps to Power." *Faith At Work News*. Reprint. 1983.

————. *Twice-Born Ministers*. New York: Fleming H. Revell, 1929.

————. *Under New Management*. Grand Rapids: Zondervan Publishing House., 1966.

————. *What the Church Has to Learn from Alcoholics Anonymous*. Reprint of 1956 sermon. Available at A.A. Archives, New York.

————. *With the Holy Spirit and with Fire*. New York: Harper & Brothers, 1960.

*A Guide to Calvary Episcopal Church: 125th Anniversary 1855-1980*. Pittsburgh: Calvary Episcopal Church, 1980.

"Buchman Religion Explained to 1,000." *New York Times*. May 27, 1931.

"Calvary Mission." Pamphlet. New York: Calvary Episcopal Church, n.d.

"Campus Calls by Dr. Shoemaker Foster Chain of Religious Cells." *New York Tribune*. February 25, 1951.

*Centennial History: Calvary Episcopal Church, 1855-1955*. Pittsburgh: Calvary Episcopal Church, 1955.

"Church Ejects Buchman Group." *New York Times*. November 8, 1941.

"Crusaders of Reform." *Princeton Alumni Weekly*. June 2, 1993.

Cuyler, John Potter, Jr. *Calvary Church in Action*. New York: Fleming H. Revell, 1934.

Day, Sherwood S. "Always Ready: S.M.S. As a Friend." *The Evangel* (New York: Calvary Church, July-August, 1950).

*Get Changed; Get Together; Get Going: A History of the Pittsburgh Experiment.* Pittsburgh: The Pittsburgh Experiment, n.d.

Harris, Irving. *The Breeze of the Spirit.* New York: The Seabury Press, 1978.

———. "S.M.S.—Man of God for Our Time." *Faith At Work* (January-February, 1964).

"Houseparties Across the Continent." *The Christian Century.* August 23, 1933.

Knippel, Charles Taylor. *Samuel M. Shoemaker's Theological Influence on William G. Wilson's Twelve Step Spiritual Program of Recovery (Alcoholics Anonymous).* Dissertation. St. Louis University, 1987.

"Listening to God Held Daily Need." *New York Times.* December 4, 1939.

Norton-Taylor, Duncan. "Businessmen on Their Knees." *Fortune.* October, 1953.

Olsson, Karl A. "The History of Faith at Work" (five parts). *Faith at Work News.* 1982-1983.

Peale, Norman Vincent. "The Unforgettable Sam Shoemaker." *Faith At Work.* January, 1964.

———. "The Human Touch: The Estimate of a Fellow Clergyman and Personal Friend." *The Evangel* (New York: Calvary Church, July-August, 1950).

Pitt, Louis W. "New Life, New Reality: A Brief Picture of S.M.S.'s Influence in the Diocese of New York." *Faith at Work*, July-August, 1950.

"Pittsburgh Man of the Year." *Pittsburgh Post Gazette.* January 12, 1956.

Sack, David Edward. *Sam Shoemaker and the "Happy Ethical Pagans."* Princeton, New Jersey: paper prepared in the Department of Religion, Princeton University, June, 1993.

"Sam Shoemaker and Faith at Work." Pamphlet on file at Faith At Work, Inc., 150 S. Washington St., Suite 204, Falls Church, VA 22046.

Schwartz, Robert. "Laymen and Clergy to Join Salute to Dr. S. M. Shoemaker." *Pittsburgh Press.* December 10, 1961.

Shoemaker, Helen Smith. *I Stand by the Door.* New York: Harper & Row, 1967.

"Sees Great Revival Near." *New York Times.* September 8, 1930.

Sider, Michael J. *Taking the Gospel to the Point: Evangelicals in Pittsburgh and the Origins of the Pittsburgh Leadership Foundation.* Pittsburgh: Pittsburgh Leadership Foundation, n.d.

"Soul Clinic Depicted By Pastor in Book." *New York Times.* August 5, 1927.

"Ten of the Greatest American Preachers." *Newsweek.* March 28, 1955.

*The Pittsburgh Experiment's Groups.* Pittsburgh: The Pittsburgh Experiment, n.d.

*Tools for Christian Living.* Pittsburgh: The Pittsburgh Experiment, n.d.

"Urges Church Aid Oxford Group." *New York Times.* January 2, 1933, p. 26.

Wilson, Bill. "I Stand by the Door." *The A.A. Grapevine.* New York: The A.A. Grapevine, Inc., February, 1967.

Woolverton, John F. "Evangelical Protestantism and Alcoholism 1933-1962: Episcopalian Samuel Shoemaker, The Oxford Group and Alcoholics Anonymous." *Historical Magazine of the Protestant Episcopal Church* 52 (March, 1983).

[The reader may find additional material by or about Samuel Shoemaker, Jr., at: (1) the Maryland Historical Society, Manuscripts Division, under "Shoemaker Papers;" (2) the Princeton University Archives at Princeton University, Olden Lane, Princeton, New Jersey, in the Samuel Shoemaker alumnus file; (3) the Episcopal Church Archives in

Austin, Texas; (4) the Library of Congress, in the Ray Foote Purdy files of the Moral Re-Armament (and Oxford Group) Archives; (5) the Maryland Diocese of the Protestant Episcopal Church; (6) the Stepping Stones Archives, Bedford Hills, New York, the Shoemaker-Wilson letters; (7) the Hartford Theological Seminary Archives, Hartford, Connecticut; and (8) the parish offices of Calvary/St. George's in New York City. In addition, articles by or about Shoemaker were written in *The Calvary Evangel*, published by Calvary Episcopal Church in New York; in the *Faith at Work* magazine, 150 South Washington Street, Suite 204, Falls Church, Virginia; and in the literature of The Pittsburgh Experiment, 1802 Investment Building, Pittsburgh, Pennsylvania 15222.]

## Spiritual Literature-Non-Oxford Group

[Almost all of these books were owned, studied, recommended, and loaned to others by Dr. Bob and h is wife, Anne.]

Allen, James. *As a Man Thinketh*. New York: Peter Pauper Press, n.d.
———. *Heavenly Life*. New York: Grosset & Dunlap, n.d.
Barton, George A. *Jesus of Nazareth*. New York: The Macmillan Company, 1922.
Bode, Carl, ed. *The Portable Emerson*. New ed. New York: Penguin Books, 1981.
Brother Lawrence. *The Practice of the Presence of God*. Pennsylvania: Whitaker House, 1982.
Browne, Lewis. *This Believing World: A Simple Account of the Great Religions of Mankind*. New York: The Macmillan Co., 1935.
Carruthers, Donald W. *How to Find Reality in Your Morning Devotions*. Pennsylvania: State College, n.d.
Chambers, Oswald. *Studies in the Sermon on the Mount*. London: Simpkin, Marshall, Ltd., n.d.
Clark, Francis E. *Christian Endeavor in All Lands*. N.p.: The United Society of Christian Endeavor, 1906.
Clark, Glenn. *Clear Horizons*. Vol 2. Minnesota: Macalester Park Publishing, 1941.
———. *Fishers of Men*. Boston: Little, Brown, 1928.
———. *God's Reach*. Minnesota: Macalester Park Publishing, 1951.
———. *How to Find Health through Prayer*. New York: Harper & Brothers, 1940.
———. *I Will Lift Up Mine Eyes*. New York: Harper & Brothers, 1937.
———. *Stepping Heavenward: The Spiritual Journal of Louise Miles Clark*. Minnesota: Macalester Park Publishing, 1940.
———. *The Lord's Prayer and Other Talks on Prayer from The Camps Farthest Out*. Minnesota: Macalester Publishing Co., 1932.
———. *The Man Who Talks with Flowers*. Minnesota: Macalester Park Publishing, 1939.
———. *The Soul's Sincere Desire*. Boston: Little, Brown, 1925.
———. *Touchdowns for the Lord. The Story of "Dad" A. J. Elliott*. Minnesota: Macalester Park Publishing Co., 1947.
———. *Two or Three Gathered Together*. New York: Harper & Brothers, 1942.
Daily, Starr. *Recovery*. Minnesota: Macalester Park Publishing, 1948.
Eddy, Mary Baker. *Science and Health with Key to the Scriptures*. Boston: Published by the Trustees under the Will of Mary Baker G. Eddy, 1916.

Fillmore, Charles. *Christian Healing*. Kansas City: Unity School of Christianity, 1936.

———, and Cora Fillmore. *Teach Us To Pray*. Lee's Summit, Missouri: Unity School of Christianity, 1950.

Fosdick, Harry Emerson. *A Great Time to Be Alive*. New York: Harper & Brothers, 1944.

———. *As I See Religion*. New York: Grosset & Dunlap, 1932.

———. *On Being a Real Person*. New York: Harper & Brothers, 1943.

———. *The Man from Nazareth*. New York: Harper & Brothers, 1949.

———. *The Manhood of the Master*. London: Student Christian Association, 1924.

———. *The Meaning of Faith*. New York: The Abingdon Press, 1917.

———. *The Meaning of Prayer*. New York: Association Press, 1915.

———. *The Meaning of Service*. London: Student Christian Movement, 1921.

Fox, Emmet. *Alter Your Life*. New York: Harper & Brothers, 1950.

———. *Find and Use Your Inner Power*. New York: Harper & Brothers, 1937.

———. *Power through Constructive Thinking*. New York: Harper & Brothers, 1932.

———. *Sparks of Truth*. New York: Grosset & Dunlap, 1941.

———. *The Sermon on the Mount*. New York: Harper & Row, 1934.

———. Pamphlets: *Getting Results by Prayer* (1933); *The Great Adventure* (1937); *You Must Be Born Again* (1936).

Glover, T. R. *The Jesus of History*. New York: Association Press, 1930.

Gordon, S. D. *The Quiet Time*. London: Fleming, n.d.

Heard, Gerald. *A Preface to Prayer*. New York: Harper & Brothers, 1944.

Herman, E. *Creative Prayer*. London: James Clarke & Co., circa 1921.

Hickson, James Moore. *Heal the Sick*. London: Methuen & Co., 1925.

James, William. *The Varieties of Religious Experience.* New York: First Vintage Press/The Library of America Edition, 1990.

Jones, E. Stanley. *Abundant Living*. New York: Cokesbury Press, 1942.

———. *Along the Indian Road*. New York: Abingdon Press, 1939.

———. *Christ and Human Suffering*. New York: Abingdon Press, 1930.

———. *Christ at the Round Table*. New York: Abingdon Press, 1928.

———. *The Choice Before Us*. New York: Abingdon Press, 1937.

———. *The Christ of Every Road*. New York: Abingdon Press, 1930.

———. *The Christ of the American Road*. New York: Abingdon-Cokesbury Press, 1944.

———. *The Christ of the Indian Road*. New York: Abingdon Press, 1925.

———. *The Christ of the Mount*. New York: Abingdon Press, 1930.

———. *Victorious Living*. New York: Abingdon Press, 1936.

———. *Way to Power and Poise*. New York: Abingdon Press, 1949.

Jung, Dr. Carl G. *Modern Man in Search of a Soul*. New York: Harcourt Brace Jovanovich, 1933.

Kagawa, Toyohiko. *Love: The Law of Life*. Philadelphia: The John C. Winston Company, 1929.

Kempis, Thomas à. *The Imitation of Christ*. Georgia: Mercer University Press, 1989.

Laubach, Frank. *Prayer (Mightiest Force in the World)*. New York: Fleming H. Revell, 1946.

Layman, Charles M. *A Primer of Prayer*. Nashville: Tidings, 1949.

Lieb, Frederick G. *Sight Unseen*. New York: Harper & Brothers, 1939.

Ligon, Ernest M. *Psychology of a Christian Personality*. New York: Macmillan, 1935.

Link, Dr. Henry C. *The Rediscovery of Man*. New York: Macmillan, 1939.

Lupton, Dilworth. *Religion Says You Can*. Boston: The Beacon Press, 1938.

Moseley, J. Rufus. *Perfect Everything*. Minnesota: Macalester Publishing Co., 1949.

Oursler, Fulton. *Happy Grotto*. Declan and McMullen, 1948.

————. *The Greatest Story Ever Told*. New York: Doubleday, 1949.

Parker, William R., and Elaine St. Johns. *Prayer Can Change Your Life*. New ed. New York: Prentice Hall, 1957.

Peale, Norman Vincent. *The Art of Living*. New York: Abingdon-Cokesbury Press, 1937.

Rawson, F. L. *The Nature of True Prayer*. Chicago: The Marlowe Company, n.d.

Sheean, Vincent. *Lead Kindly Light*. New York: Random House, 1949.

Sheen, Fulton J. *Peace of Soul*. New York: McGraw Hill, 1949.

Sheldon, Charles M. *In His Steps*. Nashville, Broadman Press, 1935.

Silkey, Charles Whitney. *Jesus and Our Generation*. Chicago: University of Chicago Press, 1925.

Speer, Robert E.. *Studies of the Man Christ Jesus*. New York: Fleming H. Revell, 1896.

Stalker, James. *The Life of Jesus Christ*. New York: Fleming H. Revell, 1891.

*The Confessions of St. Augustine*. Translated by E. B. Pusey. A Cardinal Edition. New York: Pocket Books, 1952.

*The Fathers of the Church*. New York: CIMA Publishing, 1947.

Trine, Ralph Waldo. *In Tune with the Infinite*. New York: Thomas H. Crowell, 1897.

————. *The Man Who Knew*. New York: Bobbs Merrill, 1936.

Troward, Thomas. *The Edinburgh Lectures on Mental Science*. N.p., n.d.

Uspenskii, Peter D. *Tertium Organum*. New York: A.A. Knopf, 1922.

Weatherhead, Leslie D. *Discipleship*. New York: Abingdon Press, 1934.

————. *How Can I Find God?* New York: Fleming H. Revell, 1934.

————. *Psychology and Life*. New York: Abingdon Press, 1935.

Wells, Amos R. *Expert Endeavor: A Text-book of Christian Endeavor Methods and Principles*. Boston: United Society of Christian Endeavor, 1911.

Werber, Eva Bell. *Quiet Talks with the Master*. L.A.: De Vorss & Co., 1942.

Williams, R. Llewelen, *God's Great Plan, a Guide to the Bible*. Hoverhill Destiny Publishers, n.d.

Willitts, Ethel R. *Healing in Jesus Name*. Chicago: Ethel R. Willitts Evangelists, 1931.

Worcester, Elwood, Samuel McComb, and Isador H. Coriat. *Religion and Medicine: The Moral Control of Nervous Disorders*. New York: Moffat, Yard & Company, 1908.

# Dick B.'s Historical Titles on Early A.A.'s Spiritual Roots and Successes

## *Dr. Bob and His Library: A Major A.A. Spiritual Source* (Third Edition)

Foreword by Ernest Kurtz, Ph.D., Author, *Not-God: A History of Alcoholics Anonymous*.
A study of the immense spiritual reading of the Bible, Christian literature, and Oxford Group books done and recommended by A.A. co-founder, Dr. Robert H. Smith. Paradise Research Publications, Inc.; 156 pp.; 6 x 9; perfect bound; $15.95; 1998; ISBN 1-885803-25-7.

## *Anne Smith's Journal, 1933-1939: A.A.'s Principles of Success* (Third Edition)

Foreword by Robert R. Smith, son of Dr. Bob & Anne Smith; co-author, *Children of the Healer*.
Dr. Bob's wife, Anne, kept a journal in the 1930's from which she shared with early AAs and their families ideas from the Bible and the Oxford Group. Her ideas substantially influenced A.A.'s program. Paradise Research Publications, Inc.; 180 pp.; 6 x 9; perfect bound; 1998; $16.95; ISBN 1-885803-24-9.

## *The Oxford Group & Alcoholics Anonymous* (Second Edition)

Foreword by Rev. T. Willard Hunter; author, columnist, Oxford Group activist.
A comprehensive history of the origins, principles, practices, and contributions to A.A. of "A First Century Christian Fellowship" (also known as the Oxford Group) of which A.A. was an integral part in the developmental period between 1931 and 1939. Paradise Research Publications, Inc.; 432 pp.; 6 x 9; perfect bound; 1998; $17.95; ISBN 1-885803-19-2. (Previous title: *Design for Living*).

## *The Akron Genesis of Alcoholics Anonymous* (Newton Edition)

Foreword by former U.S. Congressman John F. Seiberling of Akron, Ohio.
The story of A.A.'s birth at Dr. Bob's Home in Akron on June 10, 1935. Tells what early AAs did in their meetings, homes, and hospital visits; what they read; how their ideas developed from the Bible, Oxford Group, and Christian literature. Depicts roles of A.A. founders and their wives; Henrietta Seiberling; and T. Henry Williams. Paradise Research Pub.; 400 pp., 6 x 9; perfect bound; 1998; $17.95; ISBN 1-885803-17-6.

## *The Books Early AAs Read for Spiritual Growth* (Fwd. by John Seiberling; 7th Ed.)

The most exhaustive bibliography (with brief summaries) of all the books known to have been read and recommended for spiritual growth by early AAs in Akron and on the East Coast. Paradise Research Publications, Inc.; 126 pp.; 6 x 9; perfect bound; 1998; $15.95; ISBN 1-885803-26-5.

## *New Light on Alcoholism: The A.A. Legacy from Sam Shoemaker*

Forewords by Nickie Shoemaker Haggart, daughter of Rev. Sam Shoemaker; and Mrs. W. Irving Harris.
A comprehensive history and analysis of the all-but-forgotten specific contributions to A.A. spiritual principles and practices by New York's famous Episcopal preacher, the Rev. Dr. Samuel M. Shoemaker, Jr.—dubbed by Bill W. a "co-founder" of A.A. and credited by Bill as the well-spring of A.A.'s spiritual recovery ideas. Good Book Publishing Company; 416 pp.; 6 x 9; perfect bound; 1994; $19.95; ISBN 1-881212-06-8.

## *The Good Book and The Big Book: A.A.'s Roots in the Bible* (Bridge Builders Ed.)

Foreword by Robert R. Smith, son of Dr. Bob & Anne Smith; co-author, *Children of the Healer*.
The author shows conclusively that A.A.'s program of recovery came primarily from the Bible. This is a history of A.A.'s biblical roots as they can be seen in A.A.'s Big Book, Twelve Steps, and Fellowship. Paradise Research Publications, Inc.; 264 pp.; 6 x 9; perfect bound; 1997; $17.95; ISBN 1-885803-16-8.

## *That Amazing Grace: The Role of Clarence and Grace S. in Alcoholics Anonymous*

Foreword by Harold E. Hughes, former U.S. Senator from, and Governor of, Iowa.
Precise details of early A.A.'s spiritual practices—from the recollections of Grace S., widow of A.A. pioneer, Clarence S. Paradise Research Pub; 160 pp.; 6 x 9; perfect bound; 1996; $16.95; ISBN 1-885803-06-0.

## *Good Morning!: Quiet Time, Morning Watch, Meditation, and Early A.A.*

A practical guide to Quiet Time—considered a "must" in early A.A. Discusses biblical roots, history, helpful books, and how to. Paradise Research Pub; 154 pp.; 6 x 9; perfect bound; 1998; $15.50; ISBN: 1-885803-09-5.

## *Turning Point: A History of Early A.A.'s Spiritual Roots and Successes*

Foreword by Paul Wood, Ph.D., President, National Council on Alcoholism and Drug Dependence.
*Turning Point* is a comprehensive history of early A.A.'s spiritual roots and successes. It is the culmination of six years of research, traveling, and interviews. Dick B.'s latest title shows specifically what the Twelve Step pioneers borrowed from: (1) The Bible; (2) The Rev. Sam Shoemaker's teachings; (3) The Oxford Group; (4) Anne Smith's Journal; and (5) meditation periodicals and books, such as *The Upper Room*. Paradise Research Publications, Inc.; 776 pp.; 6 x 9; perfect bound; 1997; $29.95; ISBN: 1-885803-07-9.

Inquiries, orders, and requests for
catalogs and discount schedules
should be addressed to:

Dick B.
c/o Good Book Publishing Company
Box 837
Kihei, Maui, Hawaii 96753-0837
1-808-874-4876 (phone & fax)
email: dickb@dickb.com
Internet Web Site: "http://www.dickb.com"

# About the Author

Dick B. writes books on the spiritual roots of Alcoholics Anonymous. They show how the basic and highly successful biblical ideas used by early AAs can be valuable tools for success in today's A.A. His research can also help the religious and recovery communities work more effectively with alcoholics, addicts, and others involved in Twelve Step programs.

The author is an active, recovered member of A.A.; a retired attorney; and a Bible student. He has sponsored more than seventy men in their recovery from alcoholism. Consistent with A.A.'s traditions of anonymity, he uses the pseudonym "Dick B."

He has had thirteen titles published: *Dr. Bob's Library*; *Anne Smith's Journal, 1933-1939*; *Design for Living: The Oxford Group's Contribution to Early A.A.*; *The Akron Genesis of Alcoholics Anonymous*; *The Books Early AAs Read for Spiritual Growth*; *New Light on Alcoholism: The A.A. Legacy from Sam Shoemaker*; *Courage to Change* (with Bill Pittman); *The Good Book and The Big Book: A.A.'s Roots in the Bible*; *That Amazing Grace: The Role of Clarence and Grace S. in Alcoholics Anonymous*; *Good Morning!: Quiet Time, Morning Watch, Meditation, and Early A.A.*; *Turning Point: A History of Early A.A.'s Spiritual Roots and Successes*, *Hope!: The Story of Geraldine D., Alina Lodge & Recovery*, and *Utilizing Early A.A.'s Spiritual Roots for Recovery Today*. The books have been the subject of newspaper articles, and have been reviewed in *Library Journal*, *Bookstore Journal*, *For a Change*, *The Living Church*, *Faith at Work*, *Sober Times*, *Episcopal Life*, *Recovery News*, *Ohioana Quarterly*, *The PHOENIX*, *MRA Newsletter*, and the *Saint Louis University Theology Digest*.

Dick is the father of two married sons (Ken and Don) and a grandfather. As a young man, he did a stint as a newspaper reporter. He attended the University of California, Berkeley, where he received his A.A. degree, majored in economics, and was elected to Phi Beta Kappa in his Junior year. In the United States Army, he was an Information-Education Specialist. He received his A.B. and J.D. degrees from Stanford University, and was Case Editor of the Stanford Law Review. Dick became interested in Bible study in his childhood Sunday School and was much inspired by his mother's almost daily study of Scripture. He joined, and was president of, a Community Church affiliated with the United Church of Christ. By 1972, he was studying the origins of the Bible and began traveling abroad in pursuit of that subject. In 1979, he became much involved in a Biblical research, teaching, and fellowship ministry. In his community life, he was president of a merchants' council, Chamber of Commerce, church retirement center, and homeowners' association. He served on a public district board and was active in a service club.

In 1986, he was felled by alcoholism, gave up his law practice, and began recovery as a member of the Fellowship of Alcoholics Anonymous. In 1990, his interest in A.A.'s Biblical/Christian roots was sparked by his attendance at A.A.'s International Convention in Seattle. He has traveled widely; researched at archives, and at public and seminary libraries; interviewed scholars, historians, clergy, A.A. "old-timers" and survivors; and participated in programs on A.A.'s roots.

The author is the owner of Good Book Publishing Company and has several works in progress. Much of his research and writing is done in collaboration with his older son, Ken, who holds B.A., B.Th., and M.A. degrees. Ken has been a lecturer in New Testament Greek at a Bible college and a lecturer in Fundamentals of Oral Communication at San Francisco State University. Ken is a computer specialist.

Dick is a member of the American Historical Association, Maui Writers Guild, and The Authors' Guild. He is available for conferences, panels, seminars, and interviews.

# How to Order Dick B.'s Historical Titles on Early A.A.

## Order Form

Qty.

**Send:**

| | | |
|---|---|---|
| __ *Turning Point* (a comprehensive history) | @ $29.95 ea. | $_____ |
| __ *New Light on Alcoholism* (Sam Shoemaker) | @ $19.95 ea. | $_____ |
| __ *The Oxford Group & Alcoholics Anonymous* | @ $17.95 ea. | $_____ |
| __ *The Good Book and The Big Book* (Bible roots) | @ $17.95 ea. | $_____ |
| __ *The Akron Genesis of Alcoholics Anonymous* | @ $17.95 ea. | $_____ |
| __ *That Amazing Grace* (Clarence and Grace S.) | @ $16.95 ea. | $_____ |
| __ *Good Morning!* (Quiet Time, etc.) | @ $16.95 ea. | $_____ |
| __ *Anne Smith's Journal, 1933-1939* | @ $16.95 ea. | $_____ |
| __ *Books Early AAs Read for Spiritual Growth* | @ $15.95 ea. | $_____ |
| __ *Dr. Bob and His Library* | @ $15.95 ea. | $_____ |

*Shipping and Handling* (S & H) **          Subtotal  $_____

Add 10% of retail price (minimum US$3.75). ** U.S. only.
For "The Set," add US$18.67. ** U.S. only          **S & H**  $_____
Please call, fax, or email for shipments outside the U.S.

Total Enclosed  $_____

Name: _____ (as it appears on your credit card)

Address: _____

City: _____ State: ___ Zip: _____

Credit Card #: _____ (MC VISA AMEX) **Exp.** ____

Tel. #: _____ Signature _____

Email address: _____

## Special Value for You!

If purchased separately, the author's ten titles sell for US$186.70, plus Shipping and Handling. Using this Order Form, you may purchase sets of all ten titles for **only $149.95 per set, plus US$18.67** Shipping and Handling. Please contact us for Shipping and Handling charges for orders being shipped outside of the United States.

**Send Order Form** (or copy), with check or money order, to: Dick B., P.O. Box 837, Kihei, HI 96753-0837. Please make check or money order payable to "**Dick B.**" in U.S. dollars drawn on a U.S. bank. For questions, please phone or fax: 1-808-874-4876. Our email: dickb@dickb.com. **Dick B.'s Web Site**: "http://www.dickb.com".